DATE DUE

12/91

ROSE KENNEDY

THE CHELSEA HOUSE LIBRARY OF BIOGRAPHY

ROSE KENNEDY

SUSAN BEALE SIMONELLI

Chelsea House Publishers

New York • Philadelphia

CHELSEA HOUSE PUBLISHERS

Editor-in-Chief   Remmel Nunn
Managing Editor   Karyn Gullen Browne
Copy Chief   Mark Rifkin
Picture Editor   Adrian Allen
Art Director   Maria Epes
Assistant Art Director   Noreen Romano
Manufacturing Director   Gerald Levine
Systems Manager   Lindsey Ottman
Production Manager   Joseph Romano
Production Coordinator   Marie Claire Cebrián

The Chelsea House Library of Biography
Senior Editor   Kathy Kuhtz

*Staff for **ROSE KENNEDY***
Associate Editor   Scott Prentzas
Copy Editor   Christopher Duffy
Editorial Assistant   Tamar Levovitz
Picture Researcher   Wendy P. Wills
Designer   Basia Niemczyc
Cover Illustration   Alan Nahigian

Library of Congress Cataloging-in-Publication Data

Simonelli, Susan Beale.
Rose Kennedy/Susan Beale Simonelli.
    p.   cm.—(The Chelsea House library of biography)
Includes bibliographical references and index.
Summary: A biography of Rose Kennedy describing her family life as well as her involvement in American politics.
ISBN 0-7910-1622-6
        0-7910-1629-3 (pbk.)
1. Kennedy, Rose Fitzgerald, 1890– . —Juvenile literature. 2. Kennedy family—Juvenile literature. 3. Presidents—United States—Mothers—Biography—Juvenile literature. [1. Kennedy, Rose Fitzgerald, 1890– . 2. Presidents—Mothers. 3. Kennedy family.] I. Title. II. Series.
E748.K378S56 1991   91-7817
973.9'092—dc20   CIP
[B]   AC

Contents

THE CHELSEA HOUSE LIBRARY OF BIOGRAPHY

Barbara Bush

Clarence Darrow

Anne Frank

Raisa Gorbachev

Saddam Hussein

Rose Kennedy

Jack London

Edward R. Murrow

Edgar Allan Poe

Norman Schwarzkopf

Frank Lloyd Wright

Brigham Young

Other titles in the series are forthcoming.

Introduction

Learning from Biographies

Vito Perrone

The oldest narratives that exist are biographical. Much of what we know, for example, about the Pharaohs of ancient Egypt, the builders of Babylon, the philosophers of Greece, the rulers of Rome, the many biblical and religious leaders who provide the base for contemporary spiritual beliefs, has come to us through biographies—the stories of their lives. Although an oral tradition was long the mainstay of historically important biographical accounts, the oral stories making up this tradition became by the 1st century A.D. central elements of a growing written literature.

In the 1st century A.D., biography assumed a more formal quality through the work of such writers as Plutarch, who left us more than 500 biographies of political and intellectual leaders of Rome and Greece. This tradition of focusing on great personages lasted well into the 20th century and is seen as an important means of understanding the history of various times and places. We learn much, for example, from Plutarch's writing about the collapse of the Greek city-states and about the struggles in Rome over the justice and the constitutionality of a world empire. We also gain considerable understanding of the definitions of morality and civic virtue and how various common men and women lived out their daily existence.

Not surprisingly, the earliest American writing, beginning in the 17th century, was heavily biographical. Those Europeans who came to America were dedicated to recording their experience, especially the struggles they faced in building what they determined to be a new culture. John Norton's *Life and Death of John Cotton*, printed in 1630, typifies these early works. Later biographers often tackled more ambitious projects. Cotton Mather's *Magnalia Christi Americana*, published in 1702, accounted for the lives of more than 70 ministers and political leaders. In addition, a biographical literature around the theme of Indian captivity had considerable popularity. Soon after the American Revolution and the organization of the United States of America, Americans were treated to a large outpouring of biographies about such figures as Benjamin Franklin, George Washington, Thomas Jefferson, and Aaron Burr, among others. These particular works served to build a strong sense of national identity.

Among the diverse forms of historical literature, biographies have been over many centuries the most popular. And in recent years interest in biography has grown even greater, as biography has gone beyond prominent government figures, military leaders, giants of business, industry, literature, and the arts. Today we are treated increasingly to biographies of more common people who have inspired others by their particular acts of courage, by their positions on important social and political issues, or by their dedicated lives as teachers, town physicians, mothers, and fathers. Through this broader biographical literature, much of which is featured in the CHELSEA HOUSE LIBRARY OF BIOGRAPHY, our historical understandings can be enriched greatly.

What makes biography so compelling? Most important, biography is a human story. In this regard, it makes of history something personal, a narrative with which we can make an intimate connection. Biographers typically ask us as readers to accompany them on a journey through the life of another person, to see some part of the world through another's eyes. We can, as a result, come to understand what it is like to live the life of a slave, a farmer, a textile worker, an engineer, a poet, a president—in a sense, to walk in another's shoes. Such experience can be personally invaluable. We cannot ask for a better entry into historical studies.

Although our personal lives are likely not as full as those we are reading about, there will be in most biographical accounts many common experiences. As with the principal character of any biography, we are also faced with numerous decisions, large and small. In the midst of living our lives we are not usually able to comprehend easily the significance of our daily decisions or grasp easily their many possible consequences, but we can gain important insights into them by seeing the decisions made by others play themselves out. We can learn from others.

Because biography is a personal story, it is almost always full of surprises. So often, the personal lives of individuals we come across historically are out of view, their public personas masking who they are. It is through biography that we gain access to their private lives, to the acts that define who they are and what they truly care about. We see their struggles within the possibilities and limitations of life, gaining insight into their beliefs, the ways they survived hardships, what motivated them, and what discouraged them. In the process we can come to understand better our own struggles.

As you read this biography, try to place yourself within the subject's world. See the events as that person sees them. Try to understand why the individual made particular decisions and not others. Ask yourself if you would have chosen differently. What are the values or beliefs that guide the subject's actions? How are those values or beliefs similar to yours? How are they different from yours? Above all, remember: You are engaging in an important historical inquiry as you read a biography, but you are also reading a literature that raises important personal questions for you to consider.

Rose Kennedy poses with her husband, Joseph, her son John, and his wife, Jacqueline, soon after John won the 1960 presidential election. Rose and Joseph beam with pride over the achievement of their son, who became the nation's first Roman Catholic president.

1

Inauguration Day

ON THE MORNING OF JANUARY 20, 1961, Washington, D.C., was nearly paralyzed by eight inches of snow that a winter storm had dumped on the city the previous day. Cars and taxis were stranded on the streets, and hundreds of workmen were furiously plowing the snow on Pennsylvania Avenue. The snowfall, a blizzard by local standards, could not have struck the nation's capital at a worse time, because it was inauguration day. Tens of thousands of people, including hundreds of dignitaries from all over the world, were congregating in the city to watch John Fitzgerald Kennedy take the presidential oath.

The Kennedy family had rented a house in Georgetown, the oldest section of Washington, for a week filled with inaugural preparations and parties. Like all of the roads in the capital, the tree-lined, cobblestone streets of Georgetown were buried in snow. Despite the severe weather, 70-year-old Rose Fitzgerald Kennedy was determined to attend a special mass that morning observing her son's inauguration.

She decided that the best way to get to Holy Trinity Catholic Church was to set out on foot.

Rose, whose impeccable sense of style was well known, was not concerned about projecting an image of high fashion as she dressed for mass. To protect herself against the deep snow and the frigid air during the half-mile walk, she slipped on a pair of boots and cloaked herself in a heavy coat and several scarves. Because the sidewalks were impassable, Rose set off down the middle of the street toward Holy Trinity Church. As she approached the old white clapboard church, she noticed a group of police officers standing outside the building and several un-marked cars that she suspected were occupied by Secret Service agents. Rose later recorded in her memoirs, *Times to Remember* (1974): "Suddenly it occurred to me that Jack [the family's name for John] must be coming there for Mass."

Rose entered the church and took a seat near the back. A few minutes later, John Kennedy appeared and sat in one of the pews near the altar. Rose, a devout Roman Catholic, described in her memoirs how pleased she was that John "was there of his own volition: that he wanted to start his presidency by offering his mind and heart, and expressing his hopes and fears, to Almighty God, and asking His blessing as he began his great duties."

Kennedy did not see his mother sitting in the back of the church, but she wanted it that way. Rose knew that if she joined her son, photographers would jump to take pictures of the two of them together. She recalled that "bundled up as I was in my scarves and galoshes, I just followed the Mass and, from a distance, looked at him very happily. I wanted no picture taken of him with me in my regalia."

After the services ended, Rose did not approach John, and she quickly left the church to avoid making a fuss and attracting the news photographers. She did, however, want a ride back to the house in Georgetown so she could get a head start on the preparations for the inauguration. As she described in her memoirs, Rose approached a Secret Service agent who had accompanied her son to mass and explained, "I am Mrs. Kennedy, the President's mother. Will you please have someone come with a car and pick me up and take me to my house?" The agent nodded politely, but a car never came. "Evidently," Rose deduced, "he thought I was either an impostor or demented—because I certainly didn't look like a President's mother." Rose had to walk back to the house, but being accustomed to harsh New England winters, she did not view the journey as a hardship.

That afternoon, she watched with pride as her son stood ready to take the oath to become the 35th president of the United States. His 1960 presidential campaign had been remarkable because few men had sought the nation's highest elected office at so young an age—43. Kennedy's critics expressed many reasons why he should not run for the office of president, including his age, his relative lack of experience in government, his weak support among the national leaders of the Democratic party, and his religion.

Kennedy's career in politics had begun in 1946, when he was elected—at age 29—U.S. congressman from the Eleventh District of Massachusetts, the same district that Rose's father, John Francis Fitzgerald, had represented 50 years earlier. In 1952, Massachusetts voters elected Kennedy a U.S. senator.

John's accomplishments would not have been possible if Rose and her husband, Joseph P. Kennedy, known as Joe, had not provided him with considerable financial and emotional support. Rose's keen knowledge of Boston's precinct politics, her brilliant public speaking ability, and her appeal to women voters played a vital role in each of John's victories. Joe Kennedy, an astute and highly successful businessman, donated a substantial amount of money to his son's campaigns. He also called on his high-level business associates and influential friends to solicit contributions and to enlist their support.

Strolling through wintry Washington, D.C., on inauguration day in 1961, President John Kennedy and First Lady Jacqueline Kennedy make their way to the inaugural parade. That same morning, Rose Kennedy trudged through eight inches of snow to attend a special mass observing her son's inauguration.

Rose's energy and enthusiasm increased with each of John's campaigns. During his 1946 campaign for election to the U.S. House of Representatives, Rose spoke at hundreds of functions, either stalling the crowds until her son arrived to deliver his speech or taking over completely when John could not make an appearance. During John's successful campaign against incumbent U.S. senator Henry Cabot Lodge II in 1952, Rose hosted about 30 formal teas throughout Massachusetts. And after John secured the Democratic party's nomination for president in 1960, Rose quickly announced: "I'll go wherever they want me to go and do whatever they want me to do during the campaign."

In her memoirs, Rose described the period between John's nomination for president at the Democratic convention in July 1960 and his inauguration in January 1961 as "perhaps the busiest, most exciting months of our lives." During the 4-month presidential campaign, Rose traveled to 14 states and made 46 appearances. She always captivated audiences with her stylish, youthful looks and with her commitment to her family. Rose gained a national reputation for projecting beauty, poise, and political savvy.

Rose admitted in her autobiography that inauguration day was "somewhat blurred in my memory because so much was happening, with one stupendous scene following another." Rose took her place with the rest of the immediate family on the stage behind her son. As she watched John take the presidential oath, Rose felt that she and her husband "had given our country a young President whose words, manner, ideas, character, and everything else about him bespoke greatness."

Exuding an image of youth and vigor, the new president announced in his inaugural address that a new generation of Americans had accepted the responsibilities of power. Kennedy did not offer the country easy solutions but, instead, the challenge of hard work:

"Let every nation know . . . that we shall pay any price, bear any burden, meet any hardship, support any friend,

Women voters surround 29-year-old John Kennedy during his first campaign for Congress in 1946. Rose Kennedy's father, John Francis Fitzgerald, had represented the same Massachusetts district 50 years earlier.

oppose any foe, to assure the survival and success of liberty. . . . All of this will not be finished in the first one hundred days. Nor will it be finished in the first one thousand days, nor in the life of this Administration, nor even perhaps in our lifetime on this planet. But let us begin."

The new president finished his speech with an impassioned challenge to all Americans: "Ask not what your country can do for you—ask what you can do for your country."

John was not the only one of Rose's nine children to pursue a successful political career. Robert (Bobby) Kennedy served as attorney general in his brother's administration and as a U.S. senator representing New York. Edward (Teddy) Kennedy, Rose's youngest child, has served as a U.S. senator from Massachusetts since 1962.

Rose's other children have also devoted themselves to public service. Eunice Kennedy Shriver is the executive vice-president of the Joseph P. Kennedy, Jr., Foundation, a charitable organization (named after her brother) for the mentally handicapped that has donated millions of dollars to hospitals, institutions, day-care centers, and research projects. She was also a founder of the Special Olympics, which conducts organized athletic competitions for retarded children and adults. Patricia Kennedy Lawford serves as a trustee of the Joseph P. Kennedy, Jr., Foundation, and Jean Kennedy Smith founded Very Special Arts, an organization that supports arts programs for physically challenged individuals.

The fame and success of the Kennedy family, however, have been accompanied by recurrent tragedy. Four of Rose's children have met with untimely deaths, and her oldest daughter, Rosemary, is mentally handicapped and has required special care throughout her life. Rose's oldest son, Joseph, Jr., a pilot in the U.S. Navy, died in 1944 on a World War II flying mission. Just a few years later, her daughter Kathleen died in an airplane crash in southern France. Rose then lost two sons to assassins' bullets: John

Chief Justice Earl Warren administers the presidential oath of office to John Kennedy on January 21, 1961.

was killed while making a presidential visit to Dallas in 1963, and Robert was slain in Los Angeles while campaigning for the 1968 Democratic presidential nomination.

Rose's strong religious faith, formed when she was a young girl, has carried her through both the joyful and the devastating times in her life. Devotion, Rose observed in her memoirs, helped her recognize "that in sorrow we must look outward rather than inward."

The daughter of a Boston mayor, the wife of an ambassador, the mother of a president and two senators, Rose Kennedy has been in the public eye since the age of five. She is the matriarch of perhaps the most photographed, written about, and controversial family in U.S. history, and her success as a mother remains her proudest accomplishment. One of her granddaughters, Maria Shriver, once told an interviewer that she admired Rose because she had no embarrassment about saying that she wanted to make her husband happy or that her children were her first priority. When asked by one of her children what she most wanted to be remembered for, Rose replied, "A house full of love and laughter."

The Kennedy clan gathers following John's election to the presidency. Standing (left to right) are Ethel Skakel Kennedy, Stephen Smith, Jean Kennedy Smith, John Kennedy, Robert Kennedy, Patricia Kennedy Lawford, Sargent Shriver, Joan Bennett Kennedy, and Peter Lawford. Sitting (left to right) are Eunice Kennedy Shriver, Rose Kennedy, Joseph Kennedy, Jacqueline Bouvier Kennedy, and Edward Kennedy.

In the 1920s, John and Josephine Fitzgerald pause during a jaunt in Palm Beach, Florida. Rose's parents were the children of Irish immigrants who had fled Ireland during the catastrophic potato famine of the late 1840s.

2

$$\diamond$$

The Family Tree

ROSE ELIZABETH FITZGERALD was born in Boston, Massachusetts, on July 22, 1890. Her parents, John Francis and Mary Josephine Fitzgerald, named their first child after Rose's paternal grandmother, Rosanna Cox Fitzgerald, and her mother's sister, Elizabeth Hannon.

Rose's grandparents—Thomas and Rosanna Fitzgerald and Michael and Mary Ann Hannon—had joined the great wave of Irish immigration to the United States that took place in the late 1840s. In 1845, an uncontrollable fungus disease struck Ireland's potato crop, causing the hearty vegetable to rot in the ground and in storage bins. The country suffered a second crop failure in 1846, a third in 1848, and yet another in 1851. Potatoes were such a large part of the Irish diet that one out of every six Irish peasants died of starvation.

Fleeing the wretched conditions of their homeland and almost certain death, more than a fourth of the Irish population emigrated. More than 1 million pushed their way onto "coffin ships" (so named because 20 percent of the passengers died on board) and headed west across the

An Irish peasant family rests in front of its house in the 1880s. The potato famine compelled more than 1 million Irish to immigrate to the United States.

Atlantic Ocean in search of a better life and greater opportunities for their children.

The first major exodus from Ireland, consisting of the poorest farmers, occurred during the winter of 1846 and the spring of 1847. The Fitzgeralds and the Hannons arrived in the United States during the second wave of Irish immigration, which took place in 1847 and 1848. Nobody knows precisely when or in what order Rose's ancestors landed in Boston, but family legend maintains that her grandfather Thomas Fitzgerald was the last member of his family to leave Ireland. The family believes that he clung to the Fitzgeralds' ancestral land until there was absolutely no hope for survival.

Most of the Irish immigrants who settled in Boston found that their way of life had radically changed but that their living conditions had not greatly improved. When Thomas Fitzgerald arrived in Boston, the Irish made up one-third of the city's population. Boston society, which had been almost entirely Protestant and mainly of English descent, did not welcome the arrival of Irish Catholic immigrants. The city's most affluent inhabitants, often referred to as Brahmins (the name of the highest caste in Hindu society) because of their high social standing and cultivated intellect and taste, kept their close-knit families separated from outsiders.

In her memoirs, Rose credited these "proper Bostonians" as having "many admirable qualities, but they were a closed society." Boston's Brahmins controlled the banks, the insurance companies, and the big shipping and mercantile businesses. In *Rose: A Biography of Rose Kennedy* (1971), biographer Gail Cameron notes that the Brahmins considered the Irish, with their patched pants and country customs, "the scum of the earth" and "beaten men from beaten races, representing the worst failures in the struggle for existence." Irish laborers were barred from most desirable jobs, and, when seeking employment, they often faced signs such as No Irish Need Apply; and American, Scotch, Swiss or African—No Irish.

The Irish immigrants, most of whom were destitute, settled in Boston's North End slums, which were often described by such derogatory terms as *shantytowns* or *paddy-villes*. (The Brahmins had coined the slang word *paddy* from the common Irish name Patrick.) Tenement houses in the North End were built right up against each other, with little room behind them. The lack of sunlight, adequate ventilation, and heat in the haphazardly designed apartments created within them a dark, dull, and dank environment. The unhealthy conditions in the tenements fostered depression and disease, neither of which the Fitzgerald family managed to escape. Two of their 11 children died during infancy.

In the late 19th century, a family poses outside an apartment building on Salem Street in Boston's North End. Like many Irish immigrants who arrived in Boston, Rose's grandparents settled in the slums of the North End.

To survive the difficult decades after arriving in the United States, Rose's grandparents relied on strong family loyalty, hard work, and their faith in Roman Catholicism. When later asked why he declined an early opportunity to move out of Boston's North End to a farm in the Midwest, Thomas Fitzgerald listed three reasons: his wife, his relatives, and his church. He and Rosanna did not want to cut themselves off from their family, friends, and neighborhood. Relatives gave tremendous support to new immigrants, providing emotional and financial support while they adjusted to their adopted land. Stories of isolation on American farms and the overwhelming fear of uprooting his family again also contributed to Fitzgerald's decision to remain in Boston regardless of how unpleasant the living situation was in the North End.

Perhaps most important, the prospect of not having access to the counsel and spiritual aid of a parish priest troubled Fitzgerald. The Roman Catholic church was the mainstay of the Irish people during the social disruptions caused by the Great Famine. With its seasonal holy days, religious ceremonies, and festivals, the church provided Irish immigrants with much-needed solace and support and strengthened their community.

Upon arriving in the United States, Thomas Fitzgerald worked first on a farm outside Boston and then as a street peddler in the city itself for six years. In 1863, he decided to go into business with his older brother James, and they bought a small grocery and liquor store. The store prospered, enabling Fitzgerald to provide his family with ample food, a luxury few of his neighbors enjoyed. Boston became the Fitzgeralds' permanent home, remaining the center of the family's life for generations.

The Fitzgeralds' apartment at 33 Ferry Street consisted of a small kitchen and two rooms about the size of large closets. Despite such cramped quarters and virtually no privacy, the Fitzgeralds were fortunate that their apartment was located in the front of the building and on the top floor.

Unlike the apartments of so many other immigrants, sunlight and fresh air poured into their living space. Thomas Fitzgerald eventually saved enough money to buy a few apartment buildings in the North End. Although Rose's grandfather was never considered a wealthy man, he worked extremely hard, invested his money wisely, and provided well for his family.

Rose's father, John Francis Fitzgerald, was born on February 11, 1863, and he soon made his mark on the close-knit Irish community. Johnny, as he was known, was very competitive and always tried to be the best in everything that he did. When his two older brothers ridiculed his attempts to bulk up his slight physique by exercising, Johnny became determined to become an accomplished runner. He ran everywhere—to school, to the store, to work, to visit his friends. He soon outran his brothers and eventually raced against boys from all over Boston—and won. In *The Fitzgeralds and the Kennedys* (1987), historian Doris Kearns Goodwin relates how Johnny still beamed with pride over this achievement more than 50 years later. "I could always beat any of the boys," he crowed. "I was a champ."

In addition to running, Johnny excelled at swimming, dancing, singing, and public speaking. He later boasted that he had never been beaten in a potato-sack race, a frequent event at church socials. In her memoirs, Rose noted that her father even caught the greased pig at church picnics "so consistently that he was declared ineligible to compete." Rose acquired her father's resolve to "work harder than anyone else" and inspired her own children and grandchildren to do the same.

Johnny's drive for success intensified as he matured. According to Goodwin, Johnny graduated "a natural leader among his peers" from the Eliot Grammar School. Graduating from grammar school was considered an accomplishment for Irish Americans in those days. When Johnny enrolled at Eliot, he joined a class of 180 boys from 3 different primary schools. Of the 110 students who completed the second highest grade in June 1876, only 35 reappeared the following fall to finish their last year. Most dropped out of school as soon as they turned 14 years old because they needed to work to help their families financially.

At the age of 14, diploma in hand and overflowing with self-confidence, Johnny obtained a license to sell newspapers on the streets of Boston. Eager to make money, Johnny's boundless ambition and captivating charm enabled him to outshine his competitors. Whereas experienced newsboys sold papers from the same street corners each day, those starting out had to roam the streets to peddle their bundles. Johnny walked all over Boston shouting out the day's headlines, and he later claimed that he was always the first to sell his entire stack of newspapers. Because he had to wander throughout the city, Johnny saw parts of Boston that he had not seen before and he met all kinds of people. The enterprising Irish lad quickly built up a large network of customers.

Johnny eventually gained control of one of the city's most desirable and lucrative spots—a corner on Beacon and Park streets in an exclusive neighborhood known as

Elegant houses line a street in an affluent Boston neighborhood. As a newsboy, young John Fitzgerald came into contact with Boston's high society, which sparked his burning ambition to provide his family with the comforts and luxuries enjoyed by the upper class.

Beacon Hill. There he observed firsthand how the "other Boston" lived. In contrast to the dreary, brutish world of the North End slums, Beacon Hill was clean and cultured. Its quaint streets were lined with huge elm trees, and the Brahmins' houses were spacious and elegant. Gentlemen, dressed in fancy waistcoats and high hats, escorted refined ladies, who wore lace shawls and flowing silk dresses. Their way of life was civilized, not furious and desperate like that of the immigrants. This early exposure to Beacon Hill society had a lasting effect on Johnny, for many believed that he found in Beacon Hill a "world whose pleasures and privileges he would crave as long as he lived."

Johnny spent two years in the newspaper business before his mother died unexpectedly in 1879. Thomas Fitzgerald, who had also mourned the deaths of two of his children, decided that one of his sons should become a doctor to fight the illnesses that had claimed the lives of his loved ones.

Even though Johnny was not the oldest child, he was the obvious choice because of his academic ability and his burning desire to succeed. Although losing his newspaper income created a significant financial hardship for the family, Johnny entered the Boston Latin School in September 1879. In her memoirs, Rose described the Boston Latin School as "the oldest and, at least in those days, perhaps the most prestigious public high school in the country." Johnny quickly distinguished himself at Boston Latin. In addition to editing the school magazine, he played baseball and served as the captain of the football team for two years. Upon graduation, Johnny was accepted to Harvard Medical School.

In 1885, during Johnny's first year at Harvard, tragedy again struck his family. Thomas Fitzgerald died, leaving 9 surviving sons, 6 of whom were younger than 18-year-old Johnny. Because there were no sisters to care for the boys, the pastor of the parish church advised them to separate

John Fitzgerald entered the Boston Latin School in 1879. After graduating from the highly regarded school, he was accepted as a student by Harvard Medical School in 1885.

and to live in foster homes. In the late 19th century, the role of maintaining households fell on women, who did all of the cooking and cleaning and attended to the needs of the men in the family. Men rarely concerned themselves with housework. But Johnny, stubbornly defying convention and refusing to allow his family to disintegrate, dropped out of medical school and returned home to take care of his brothers.

In desperate need of a job, Johnny turned to the most powerful man in the North End for help—the neighborhood boss, Matthew Keany. Because local governments did not provide adequate social services to satisfy the urgent needs of their newest citizens, immigrants in most large U.S. cities, including the Irish in Boston, organized a system of local politics that was headed by ward bosses. In exchange for votes in future elections, ward bosses helped the immigrants survive the daily challenge of living in a strange land. For example, the boss would protect immigrants from unethical landlords and employers, help them find a job, pay for groceries if a sick or injured worker could not afford to feed his family, or pay for funeral expenses if a family could not afford them. This "machine" style of politics eventually made the Irish the dominant force in the Democratic party in Boston, New York, and Chicago.

As Doris Goodwin notes, Matthew Keany believed that Johnny had "the promise of a natural politician, with more potential than any other young man in his district." Although Keany wanted to hire Johnny as his apprentice, he felt compelled to carry out a promise he had made to Thomas Fitzgerald just before he died —that he would help Johnny become a doctor. Keany offered Johnny money for his tuition and for a housekeeper to care for his brothers. Goodwin records that Johnny, however, "was not to be driven from his decision" to get a job, and he refused the proposal. After realizing that Johnny would not change his mind, Keany offered Fitzgerald a position as his apprentice. Upon hearing that, Johnny "leaped up from his seat, threw his arms around the older man and said he'd report to work the following morning."

Under Keany, Fitzgerald studied ward politics and the complexities and interactions of family relationships and the community's social and religious organizations. He watched firsthand how Keany traded favors to gain an increasing range of influence over the community. After several months, Keany rewarded Fitzgerald's loyalty by securing him a job in the Customs House of Boston Harbor.

The "life of a custom's clerk," Rose explained in her autobiography, however, "could not contain my father's energies for long or ever satisfy his ambitious nature." Fitzgerald left the Customs House after three years to start an insurance and real estate business. Contacts from his involvement in so many civic, social, and athletic organizations in the North End, along with what Rose refers to as his "natural gifts of salesmanship," helped Fitzgerald improve his financial situation, enabling him to propose marriage to Mary Josephine Hannon.

Johnny had been in love with Josie, as she was known, for years. Her parents settled in the small town of Acton, northwest of Boston. Johnny and Josie were second cousins and first met at a family gathering in Acton when they were teenagers. To Johnny, Josie was the ideal Irish-Victorian woman. With shimmering black hair and rosy cheeks, she was a natural beauty who always carried herself erect, as proper young women of the time were taught to do. In Rose's words, "She [Josie] had dark Irish looks, with a fine complexion, and a small lithe, trim figure, which she never lost." Josie was also shy, polite, and reserved. According to the popular Catholic monthly, *Donahoe's*, these were qualities that every young Catholic woman of that era was supposed to display.

"Father was an extrovert," Rose wrote in her memoirs. "He would talk with anybody about anything. When [Josie] spoke, it was usually directly and to the point. He enjoyed being with people of all kinds [and] she was happiest with friends and close members of the family."

After a simple wedding in 1889, Johnny and Josie lived first with Johnny's brothers in the Fitzgeralds' house on Ferry Street. They moved to an apartment at 4 Garden Court, also in the North End, when Josie learned she was pregnant. As was customary in the late 19th century, Josie stayed at home to take care of the house and Johnny worked to advance his own career. Johnny hoped that the baby would be a girl, perhaps because he and his brothers grew up without a sister and had had no female in the household after their mother died.

When Rose was born on July 22, 1890, Johnny excitedly ran up and down the streets telling neighbors of the magnificent news. The moment Johnny saw his beautiful and healthy baby girl, Rose became his special joy. As she grew up, Rose idolized her father and became very much like him—vivacious, self-disciplined, well read, hardworking, athletic, and possessing a natural flair for attractive clothes and the latest fashion styles.

By the time of Rose's birth, the balance of political power in Boston had shifted dramatically from the Brahmins to the Irish. Because they had become a larger portion of the city's electorate, many Irishmen entered politics, working within the ward-boss system to protect the interests of their working-class constituents. In 1892, Johnny gave up the insurance business and won a seat on the Common Council, the lowest branch of Boston's city government. His inexhaustible energy, ability to talk on any topic to any audience, and his short, stocky, ruby-faced good looks made him popular with the voters and an integral part of the North End's political machine.

Although Fitzgerald became known as "Honey Fitz" because of his smooth speech-making ability, local cartoonists depicted him as the "Napoleon of Ward Six." He was elected to the state senate in 1893, and the following year he unseated incumbent U.S. congressman Joseph

John Fitzgerald was elected to the Massachusetts state senate in 1893 and to the U.S. House of Representatives in 1894. Honey Fitz, as Fitzgerald became known to his constituents, served in Congress for six years.

O'Neil. For the next six years, Fitzgerald traveled back and forth between Boston and Washington, D.C., representing the Eleventh District of Massachusetts in the U.S. House of Representatives. In her memoirs Rose recalled with pride how her father "was one of the youngest men in Congress, the only Democrat from the whole of New England, and the only Catholic." Fitzgerald's three-term career in Congress was undistinguished but often colorful. One of his colleagues, Representative Charles Henry Grosvenor of Ohio, remembered Fitzgerald as "always jumping around and chattering."

Regardless of what his critics might have thought about his behavior, Fitzgerald was intensely committed to preventing the enactment of restrictive immigration legislation. He felt that people of any nationality should be able to immigrate to the United States. In 1897, he helped persuade President Grover Cleveland to veto a bill that would have severely limited the number of immigrants allowed to enter the United States.

In 1897, when Rose was seven, the Fitzgeralds moved from Boston's North End to West Concord, Massachusetts. The apartment on Garden Street had become too small for the growing family, which now included Rose's younger sister, Agnes, and her brother, Thomas. Because he was away much of the time working in Washington, Johnny wanted the family's new home to be closer to Josie's relatives in Acton. The Fitzgeralds lived on Main Street in West Concord for six years and had two more children, Eunice and John Francis, Jr. Situated on a hilltop and set back from the street, their large wooden house had a huge porch, a glassed-in conservatory, and even a barn and a henhouse.

In her memoirs, Rose fondly remembered those "wonderful years, full of the traditional pleasures and satisfactions of life in a small New England town. Years of serenity, order, neighborly human relationships, family affection: trips with horse and buggy to my grandparents' house, climbing apple trees and gathering wildflowers in the woods behind the house." In a nearby pond, Johnny taught Rose and her younger siblings how to swim, an activity that remained one of the abiding pleasures in Rose's life. Every Sunday, the Fitzgeralds dressed up in their finest clothes and attended morning mass. Afterward they enjoyed what Rose notes was a "bountiful country-style noontime dinner."

Each summer, the Fitzgeralds spent two or three weeks at Old Orchard Beach, a resort town in Maine. Many of the Fitzgeralds' friends, practically all of whom were Irish

Catholics from Johnny's congressional district, also vacationed there. Among them were the Kennedys. Patrick Joseph Kennedy, a saloonkeeper and later a banker, had a reputation for being a shrewd but impeccably honest businessman. Kennedy, known as P.J., was also an influential political leader in East Boston. Most important, though, Kennedy was the father of Rose's future husband, Joseph Patrick Kennedy. An old photograph that surfaced decades later shows several families, including the Fitzgeralds and the Kennedys, enjoying a picnic in Old Orchard Beach. Although they did not remember the occasion, Rose Fitzgerald and Joe Kennedy first met at Old Orchard Beach when they were young children.

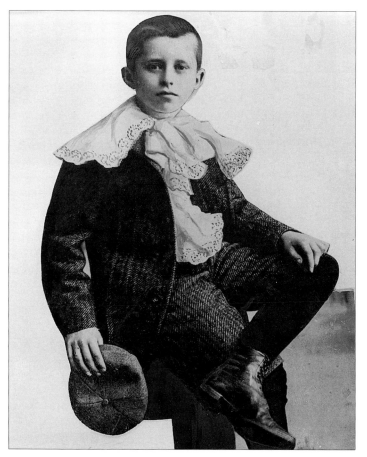

Rose Fitzgerald first met her future husband, Joseph Kennedy, at Old Orchard Beach, Maine, when they were youngsters.

In 1912, Rose Fitzgerald and her father depart for a tour of South America. Once she reached her teens, Rose often accompanied her father as he carried out his duties as mayor.

3

The Education of Miss Fitzgerald

DESPITE WHAT OTHERS MIGHT HAVE THOUGHT, Rose believed that her sister Agnes was prettier than she was. Once, when Johnny was a congressman, he took Rose and Agnes to meet President William McKinley at the White House. McKinley told Agnes that she was the most beautiful girl that he had ever seen, but he failed to compliment Rose on her appearance. Although she was only seven years old at the time, Rose always remembered what McKinley said. She later admitted, "I knew right then and there that I would have to work hard to do something about myself."

McKinley's opinion notwithstanding, Rose was a beautiful girl. Many of Rose's fellow students at the Edward Everett Grammar School in West Concord considered Rose the prettiest girl in the class. In addition to her good looks, Rose set high academic standards for herself and consistently earned straight A's. Instead of taking her privileges as the daughter of a U.S. congressman for granted, Rose constantly strove to improve herself and to make her father proud. As historian

Doris Goodwin has recorded, Rose later observed, "Some children will study less if their father is in an important position. I studied more because I thought I was more conspicuous on that account."

By the age of 12, Rose had her own rig—a small horse and carriage. She used the coach for all sorts of errands and recorded in her memoirs that she "remembers best the summer days when school was out and time was heavy and I used [the rig] to drive back and forth to the Concord Library for books." Like her father, Rose was an avid reader. She especially enjoyed books by Louisa May Alcott, who lived and wrote in Concord. The Concord Library had Alcott's complete works, and Rose read them all. Her favorite was *Little Women*, Alcott's most popular novel, about a mother who raises four strong-willed daughters by herself while her husband is away fighting in a war. The family's love and determination carries them through their trying times.

Rose was much more intellectual and ambitious than her sister Agnes. Marie Greene, a close friend of the sisters, told biographer Gail Cameron that "Agnes was not nearly so smart [as Rose] and she never tried to be." According to Greene, Agnes was also much more shy than Rose. For example, Agnes was supposed to sing at a school concert, but when she opened her mouth, not one sound came out. At the same time, though, Rose continued to play the piano perfectly.

While pushing herself to excel, Rose also encouraged her brothers and sisters to study hard and act like the sons and daughters of a prominent figure. As the Fitzgerald family grew, Rose helped her mother care for her younger siblings. According to Cameron, Rose's brother Tom once said, "What I remember most about Rosie when we were growing up was that she was always nagging me about studying Latin and playing the violin." And a classmate at Edward Everett remembers how Rose once sharply scolded Agnes for walking out of the house while eating,

Rose Fitzgerald (third from left) sits between her father (right) and P. J. Kennedy (left) at Old Orchard Beach, Maine. Like many of Boston's well-to-do Irish families, the Fitzgeralds and the Kennedys often vacationed there.

behavior that Rose found totally inappropriate for a congressman's daughter. Rose took great pride in being a politician's daughter and expected the rest of her family to follow her example.

Although Rose acquired Josie's practical and unemotional way of coping with demanding situations, it was Johnny who had the most profound influence on Rose's character. Cameron records Rose's recollection that "I found the role my father played in my life a decisive one. He talked to me incessantly, all the time I was growing up. He told me a lot about the history of the Irish people, about their culture; we discussed politics and government constantly." As soon as she was in her teens, Rose became her father's constant companion. Unlike her mother, who refrained from making public appearances, Rose loved official gatherings and made a wonderful impression on everyone she met.

Soon after an unsuccessful attempt at a fourth term in Congress in 1901, Rose's father bought a faltering weekly newspaper called *The Republic* for $500. Johnny "knew the power of the press in politics," Rose wrote in her memoirs, "and in *The Republic* he saw a potentially valuable instrument for advancing his political career." Rose's father had decided that he wanted to become the mayor of Boston.

Fitzgerald mastered the publishing business and in a short time significantly increased the paper's revenues. He later told Rose that "the success of a newspaper depended on its advertising revenue, and that advertisers look to women, who spend most of the money in the big stores. I accordingly made the paper more readable to women." In her memoirs, Rose suggested that this shrewd maneuver probably "influenced some of the campaign strategies Jack would adopt when he entered public life."

As a newspaper publisher, Fitzgerald made 5 times more money than he had earned as a congressman, which enabled him to move his family to a magnificent house in Dorchester, a wealthy and mostly Catholic suburb of Boston, when Rose was 13. Rose's youngest brother, Frederick, was born there.

Even though Fitzgerald no longer traveled back and forth to Washington, he still spent much of his time away from home. In addition to his newspaper work, Rose's father began preparing for his campaign to become mayor of Boston. He attended as many social and political functions in Boston as he could. Rose admitted in her memoirs that she was not very "happy about that, at the time," but she also realized that "this is a price that members of a 'political family' have to pay." Later, when her own husband traveled frequently on business, Rose accepted it and, according to her husband Joe, never complained.

In 1905, Johnny formally announced his candidacy for mayor of Boston in Palm Beach, Florida, where the Fitzgeralds had begun to take annual vacations. In her memoirs, Rose described her father's first mayoral race as "one of the most hard-fought, noisy, complex political melees ever seen in Boston." Fitzgerald ran for the Democratic nomination without the support of the powerful Strategy Board, a select group of Irish community leaders that included P. J. Kennedy. Fitzgerald decided to fight the "contest single-handedly," without the Strategy Board, and adopted a platform with the slogan, "Down with the bosses! The people, not the bosses, must rule!"

Doris Goodwin suggests that the real strength behind Fitzgerald's candidacy was his promise that "the gang in City Hall for four years would be cleaned out to make room for another gang." Fitzgerald secured the support of a large number of discontented politicians who had been overlooked by the administration of Mayor Patrick A. Collins.

After practically round-the-clock campaigning, Fitzgerald won the Democratic nomination. Once he gained the Democratic party's backing, Fitzgerald received the Strategy Board's support and won the general election because Republicans Louis Frothingham and Henry Dewey (who ran as an independent candidate) split their party's votes.

The election-night celebration at the Quincy House was so lively and well attended, Rose recalled in her memoirs, that "my father could not even get inside to attend his own victory party." She remembers that his loud protests, "I've just been elected mayor and they're all waiting for me. I'm John F. Fitzgerald," were to no avail. Fitzgerald had to be lifted up to an iron awning above the doorway, from which he delivered a rousing victory speech.

Although Johnny furiously attended to the business at City Hall, as Rose later noted in her memoirs, her father's "new status made little difference in our lives." Because Fitzgerald had always worked long hours and had devoted much of his free time to local politics, his family had become accustomed to publicity and the pressures associated with it.

During this exhilarating time, Rose attended Dorchester High School, where she maintained a stellar academic record and graduated in June 1906 at the age of 15. Rose was the youngest person ever to graduate from Dorchester High School and the only student to receive her diploma from her own father, who officiated at the event. A news

John Fitzgerald served two terms as mayor of Boston, from 1906 to 1907 and from 1910 to 1914. Rose idolized her father and became very much like him—vivacious, urbane, hardworking, and athletic.

William O'Connell, the influential archbishop of Boston, pressured John Fitzgerald into not allowing Rose to attend Wellesley College, a liberal—and Protestant—college that had already accepted her as a student. To mollify O'Connell, Fitzgerald enrolled his daughter in the Convent of the Sacred Heart, a Catholic college in Boston.

article reported, "much interest was manifested by the audience when [the mayor] called forward Rose Elizabeth Fitzgerald, his daughter, and handed the prized certificate to her." A picture of Rose accepting her diploma appeared on the front page of Boston's *Post*.

Rose was embarrassed, though, by what she referred to in her memoirs as the "florid tribute" that accompanied the photo. The headline read: MOST BEAUTIFUL GIRL GRADUATE? And the story that followed included such statements as "Her attractiveness surpasses that of any other graduate of the state." Rose recorded in her memoirs that she "was sure it was the worst thing that could happen to me, and all my friends would hate me." Luckily, Rose's friends correctly assumed that her boastful, good-hearted father had arranged the whole thing through one of his connections at the *Post*.

Rose was accepted to Wellesley College in her third year at Dorchester and had her heart set on starting there the fall after she completed a postgraduate, college-preparatory year of high school. Johnny, however, had other plans for Rose. He told Rose that he and her mother thought she was still too young to go away to Wellesley (20 miles from Boston), and he enrolled his daughter at the Convent of the Sacred Heart in Boston.

Rose did not protest her father's decision, but, according to Doris Goodwin, "[i]t did enter her mind that there was a betrayal in his words." Rose immediately dismissed any doubts she had about her father's intentions, but Goodwin suggests that Rose's suspicions were well founded. Johnny did not tell Rose the whole story about why she could not go to Wellesley. Goodwin claims that Johnny's decision reflected a concern for his political career rather than his daughter's education. The day before Johnny told Rose that she would be attending the convent instead of Wellesley, he had a meeting with William O'Connell, the archbishop of Boston. As a high-ranking priest who oversaw all of the parishes in Boston, O'Connell was a powerful force in Boston politics. Fitzgerald had recently lost the archbishop's backing because of an investigation during the summer of 1907 into the manner in which the mayor's newly created Supply Department had given out city contracts for coal. Fitzgerald was anxious to regain some of O'Connell's support.

Although the mayor was not personally accused of any wrongdoing, Goodwin argues that his administration's involvement in the "disgraceful hearings only reinforced O'Connell's view that with Fitzgerald the Irish were caught in an outdated mold." As Goodwin notes, O'Connell strongly believed that the typical Irish politicians in the North End would not be able to lead Irish Catholics "into a new era which would see them obtain proper dignity and genuine respect."

When Fitzgerald met with O'Connell in September 1907, one of the subjects that they discussed was the education of his daughters. Hearing that Rose was planning to go to Wellesley, a Protestant college, O'Connell became upset. Knowing how much her peers respected Rose, he was afraid other Catholic girls in the community would follow Rose's example. O'Connell strongly believed young Catholic women should be educated in Catholic schools. Eager to appease O'Connell, Fitzgerald quickly assured him that his daughter would attend the Convent of the Sacred Heart.

The convent, founded by the Society of the Sacred Heart, was one of an exclusive order of schools for daughters of well-to-do Catholic families. The purpose of the Society of the Sacred Heart, conceived by Madame Sophie Barat in France in 1800, was to prepare young women to become wives and mothers.

Rose was devastated by her father's decision about Wellesley, not because she disagreed with Sacred Heart's mission but because, in her words, "I'm sure it [Wellesley] would have been an interesting and rewarding experience." Goodwin notes that when asked at the age of 90 to describe her biggest regret, Rose responded "with a bitterness of tone she did not often allow herself to betray" that it "is not having gone to Wellesley College. It is something I have felt a little sad about all my life."

Rose quickly grew to like Sacred Heart, however, and supplemented her studies there with piano lessons at the New England Conservatory of Music. At the turn of the century, the ability to play some sort of instrument or to sing was considered a social asset. Encouraged by her parents, Rose practiced the piano for an hour and a half each day and has enjoyed playing throughout the years.

In 1907, Johnny's first term as mayor ended, and he faced another election. Although the Strategy Board was behind him from the beginning this time, Johnny did not win. Shortly before the municipal election, Johnny's campaign suffered a major blow. A longtime clerk in the Supply Department admitted that in addition to procuring coal contracts illegally during Fitzgerald's administration, the Supply Department often paid double or even triple the going rates for many other contracts. According to the clerk, the excess profits were divided between the individual contractors and the politicians who orchestrated the deals, particularly Michael Mitchell, the head of the city's Supply Department and a close friend of the mayor's. The clerk's statement became the basis for a new set of public hearings, and his testimony was released just a few days before the election. Fitzgerald lost to the Republican candidate, George A. Hibbard.

The following summer, in 1908, Johnny took Josie, Rose, and Agnes on a tour of Europe. In two months, the Fitzgeralds traveled to Ireland, England, Belgium, France, Switzerland, Germany, and Holland. At the end of the summer, Fitzgerald enrolled his two daughters in the Sacred Heart convent at Blumenthal, Holland. "In those times," Rose Kennedy wrote in her memoirs, "it was considered a great advantage for a young person to have gone to school abroad."

Back in Boston, the investigation into the Supply Department's questionable procurement practices continued. According to Goodwin, Johnny's decision to send Rose and Agnes away to school reflected his "desire to shield his daughters from the vicious struggle that lay ahead, the likelihood that he would have to take the stand against Mitchell at a public trial, or even worse, the chance that he himself might be brought into court on any of the Finance Commission's charges." Fitzgerald was never indicted on any charges, but he had to testify against Mitchell, both at a grand jury hearing and subsequently at his friend's trial.

It was a stressful time for the Fitzgeralds. The probe into Johnny's administration and the resulting trial was front-page news for months. Mitchell was found guilty of defrauding the city and sentenced to one year in prison. Johnny did not bring Rose and Agnes back from the Blumenthal convent until after the trial ended.

Like the convent Rose attended in Boston the previous year, Blumenthal was one of the convents of the Society of the Sacred Heart. It was at Blumenthal, with its rigid schedules and pious standards of duty and devotion to others, that Rose solidified her faith in Roman Catholicism. She found Blumenthal very different from the world that she knew in Boston. One of Rose's closest friends at Blumenthal later described to biographer Gail Cameron the way they felt: "At home, we had heard the worst music, and attended the ugliest churches. We had to learn the catechism by heart but had no religious feeling. Then we were transported to a world physically austere, but so beautiful we both experienced a spiritual transformation, living in a world where the chief concern was to know, to love, and to serve God."

The nuns at Blumenthal enforced strict rules for socializing, dressing, and studying. The girls were expected to be washed, dressed, and ready for assembly each morning by 6:15 A.M. sharp. During the recitation of morning prayers, the girls were obliged to join hands and keep their

eyes lowered and their backs straight. The slightest sag or
mere shuffling of one's feet could merit a bad point at the
weekly evaluation of each girl's conduct.

Like those at the Sacred Heart convent in Boston, the
class hours at Blumenthal were long, and the nuns were
demanding. And Rose had to speak and write in German
instead of English. In one of her many letters to her parents,
Rose wrote that she and Agnes "try to talk together at night
when we are getting ready for bed. We do not have much
opportunity during meals for we have conversation only
during breakfast time for a few minutes. During dinner
there is German reading, and during supper, French reading, and we are silent. I am used to this regulation now, but
at first it was very hard."

Because she worked hard at her religious studies, Rose
was accepted into the sodality of the Children of Mary of
the Sacred Heart, the highest lifelong commitment a
Sacred Heart student can make. The sodality is an association of women who promise to dedicate their lives to
following the example of the Immaculate Mother to build
their own characters and those of others and to progress
continually in their faith.

In August 1909, Johnny arrived at Blumenthal to bring
Rose and Agnes home. Before returning to Boston, he first
took them on a wonderful trip around Europe, including
stops in Amsterdam and The Hague in the Netherlands;
Brussels, Belgium; Paris; London; and Edinburgh. They
docked in Boston on August 20 and were greeted by Josie,
who, Rose reported in her memoirs, had "been terribly
lonely" without her two oldest daughters.

Eager to continue her education, Rose spent the following academic year at the Convent of the Sacred Heart in
the Manhattanville section of New York City. In a letter
home to her parents while she was still in Blumenthal, Rose
explained that "one year at day school and one year at a
foreign boarding school is not quite enough to give me all
the little charms and graces of a Sacred Heart girl."

The summer before Rose left for Manhattanville, Johnny decided to run for mayor of Boston again, and he won the Democratic nomination. In her memoirs, Rose explained that the 1909 mayoral race was the "first political campaign of any sort of which I was fully aware." Although her father "seemed to take it more or less for granted," Rose became livid at the slander and gossip the Boston newspapers printed about him. She quickly realized, however, that "denunciation and even vilification are part of the price one pays for being in public life." With a platform promising concern for the working man, Johnny beat J. J. Storrow— a man of proper Bostonian stock who was the president of the Chamber of Commerce and an overseer of Harvard College—by a slim margin of 1,402 votes.

After receiving her graduation certificate from Manhattanville and a gold medal for general excellency, Rose returned to Boston in June 1910. She noted in her memoirs that, at the age of 20, she was on the "verge of leaving girlhood." The next several years brought great adventure

In 1910, Rose Fitzgerald (standing, far right) poses with her fellow Manhattanville graduates. After returning from a Sacred Heart boarding school in Holland in 1909, Rose finished her education at the Convent of the Sacred Heart located in the Manhattanville section of the Bronx, New York.

In 1912, Mayor John Fitzgerald (center) shares a laugh with President William Howard Taft, who was in Boston campaigning for local candidates.

and much happiness to Rose. She was once again the daughter of the mayor and spent much of her time with her father. Fitzgerald took his gregarious eldest daughter to dedications, receptions, banquets, picnics, parades, rallies, grand marches, and ceremonies.

Serving as her father's companion, hostess, and assistant, Rose accompanied Johnny on most of his official trips. She went with him to Chicago for an international meeting of municipal executives and to Baltimore for the 1912 Democratic National Convention. Rose also traveled with Johnny to Panama to determine the possible effects on Boston of the recently opened Panama Canal and to Europe with a Chamber of Commerce delegation to examine such large port cities as Brussels, Belgium, and Hamburg, Germany. Fluent in French and German, Rose often served as the group's interpreter.

When she was not with her father, Rose attended classes in French, German, and art at Boston University and continued her music classes at the New England Conservatory of Music. Rose also joined a small theater group, taught catechism classes and Sunday school, attended educational lectures, and served on the Public Library Investigating

Committee, whose primary function was to recommend books appropriate for Boston schoolchildren to read. She taught sewing to a class of Italian children in the North End and became involved in a number of other civic activities, including volunteer work in settlement houses and social agencies.

Rose's social life revolved around the sons and daughters of other prominent Irish Catholics. Although some of the Irish immigrant families had achieved a level of prosperity similar to the Brahmins by the early 20th century, two separate societies still existed in Boston—one almost entirely Protestant and the other predominantly Catholic. People of the same social background met frequently in clubs. Rose noted in her memoirs that "[t]hey had their Junior League, we had our Cecilian Club equally dedicated in principle to unselfish good works." She also explains that the arrangement was "sensible" because not having Protestant boys at their dances helped "prevent romances leading to 'mixed marriages' with the eventual unhappiness that sometimes awaited such a marriage in the world as it was."

Rose herself founded an exclusive club called the Ace of Clubs, which admitted single Catholic women who had studied abroad and who were interested in discussing international affairs and current events. The purpose of the Ace of Clubs was educational rather than social. Rose was a serious young woman. She commented in her memoirs that "a life of partying and socializing would have bored me to death." Marie Greene claimed that the members of the Ace of Clubs "were all from substantial homes, and so they didn't really need the whole New England thing." Johnny Fitzgerald arranged for the eight charter members to meet in the Rose Room at the Somerset Hotel, and he often convinced visiting dignitaries to give speeches to the club.

Rose also frequently accompanied Johnny on the piano while he sang. Rose remembers that "he did a great deal of singing instead of speechifying." One of the most popular tunes of the time was "Sweet Adeline." Fitzgerald adored it and soon turned it into his political trademark. Rose claimed in her memoirs that, having played it a "few thousand" times for her father, it was "as inseparable from his legend as 'Happy Days Are Here Again'" was to Franklin D. Roosevelt.

During this time, Rose's mother, Josie, continued to remain at home most of the time tending to her family. In her autobiography, Rose claimed that Josie "appreciated" Rose's "cooperation" with her father and that she and Josie "reached a perfect arrangement" about Rose's participation in her father's affairs. Rose repeated what Josie once told an interviewer: "I am a home woman in every way, and my one ambition is to make the home the most happy and attractive place for my husband and our children." Josie was happy to let Rose fill in for her.

One public event that involved the whole family, though, was Rose's debut on Monday, January 2, 1911. It was the highlight of Rose's early social life and a triumph for Boston's Irish-Catholic society. The City Council of Boston voted to postpone its scheduled meeting that day so that all of its members could attend the most anxiously awaited event of the season—Rose Fitzgerald's debut. In that era, a young woman's debut was a rite of passage that formally introduced her to society as a prospective bride.

Wearing a beautiful white satin dress and carrying violets, which symbolized modesty, and lilies of the valley, which symbolized beauty, Rose greeted her guests on the porch of the Fitzgeralds' house. She recalled in her autobiography: "I was so excited by the occasion that I felt no fatigue standing three or four hours and shaking hands with more than 450 people, among them the new governor, two congressmen, and numerous other dignitaries."

Once again, Rose made the front page of the *Boston Post*. The reporter described Rose as having "never lost her self possession or [given] the least indication of being

After graduating from Harvard, Joseph Kennedy worked as a state bank examiner for 18 months. In 1914, he deftly saved Columbia Trust Co., Boston's only Irish-controlled bank, from a hostile takeover. In appreciation for his efforts, the directors of Columbia Trust (one of whom was P. J. Kennedy) appointed the 25-year-old Kennedy president of the bank.

tired or bored. She had pleasant words for all and a laugh that was musical." Doris Goodwin observes that Rose's debut "was considered one of the most elaborate coming-out parties ever conducted in Boston." When the formal reception was over, Rose and her friends, along with a group of young gentlemen, continued celebrating with a sumptuous dinner and then a dance. Among the guests at the dance was Joe Kennedy.

By the time she was 17, Rose knew that she was in love with Joe and that she wanted to marry him. Although Joe also loved Rose, their courtship was complicated because Johnny disapproved of the relationship. Rose claimed in her autobiography that her father loved her so much and had such "extravagant notions of my beauty, grace, wit, and charm" that no man would have been good enough for her. But many others have said that Rose's father disliked Joe because of Johnny's strained relationship with Joe's father, P. J. Kennedy. It was no secret that Fitzgerald and P.J. disagreed on many occasions, including whether Fitzgerald should have received the nomination for mayor in 1905. Furthermore, according to Gail Cameron, "Honey Fitz looked down on the Kennedys socially." Although the Kennedys and the Fitzgeralds came from similar backgrounds, Fitzgerald considered his family "one of the FIF's, First Irish Families." Johnny had already selected someone else for Rose—Hugh Nawn, the son of a wealthy building contractor and close friend and neighbor.

Rose was torn between her feelings for Joe and her loyalty to her father. She continued to see Joe discreetly and tried to hide their relationship from her parents. At dances, Rose often covered her dance card with initials of imaginary partners so that no one would know she was reserving all of her dances for Joe. She and Joe often met secretly at a friend's house in Cambridge or at the Christian Science Church in Boston, which the couple had once ducked into to avoid a photographer.

By January 1914, after serving for 18 months as a state bank examiner, Joe Kennedy was appointed president of the Columbia Trust Company, Boston's only Irish-controlled bank. At 25, Joe was one of the nation's youngest bank presidents, and Johnny could no longer object to his suitability as a husband.

On October 7, 1914, Joe and Rose were married in Archbishop O'Connell's private chapel. Their modest wedding—only the immediate families of the bride and groom were present at the early-morning mass—was followed by a wedding breakfast for about 75 guests. "Neither one of us wanted a public fiesta," Rose later wrote in her memoirs. For Rose, her marriage to Joe marked the beginning of a new "season" in her life. As she wrote in her memoirs, quoting a famous passage from Ecclesiastes, "To everything there is a season, and a time for every purpose. There was courtship, there was the discovery of love, there was engagement, there was marriage, there was parenthood: Each in its season and marked by traditions and rituals."

On October 7, 1914, newlyweds Joseph and Rose Kennedy emerge from Archbishop O'Connell's chapel. This dynamic couple would engender a large, charismatic family whose members were ambitious and competitive, as well as fiercely loyal to each other.

In 1922, Rose poses with Eunice (on lap), Kathleen, Rosemary (seated), John (on tricycle), and Joe, Jr., on the lawn of their Brookline, Massachusetts, home.

4

Rose and the Young Kennedys

AFTER A HONEYMOON AT THE GREENBRIER RESORT in White Sulphur Springs, West Virginia, Rose and Joe Kennedy returned to Boston to their new home, which they had already furnished. Although the three-story gray frame house at 83 Beals Street in Brookline, Massachusetts, would eventually become a national historical site, the newlyweds did not consider it much different from all the other houses on the block.

Rose and Joe had 7 children during the 12 years that they lived in Brookline. Their oldest son, Joseph, Jr., was born in 1915, and their second son, John, was born in 1917, the year that the United States entered World War I. Because most Americans preferred to avoid Europe's strife, the United States had remained isolated from much of the conflict, which had begun in 1914.

Life in Brookline for Rose and Joe remained simple during the early years of their marriage. Rose's chief cares centered on her children, who soon included Rosemary, born in 1919, and Kathleen, who arrived the following year. Although she enjoyed the help of a nursemaid, housekeeper, and cook, Rose managed the growing household. Rose recalled in her memoirs that she "did little diaper changing, but I had to be sure there were plenty of good-quality diapers on hand, and that they were changed as needed and properly washed and stowed for use."

Responsibility for the operation of the household fell on Rose's shoulders because Joe worked long hours and often traveled on business. Joe soon realized that his position at the bank could not help him achieve his goal of becoming a millionaire by the age of 35, so he accepted a position as the assistant general manager of Bethlehem Steel's large Fore River shipyards in Quincy, Massachusetts. Second in charge at the shipyards, Joe supervised 2,200 employees and earned an annual salary of $22,000, a remarkable sum in 1917.

The war in Europe sent a tremendous amount of business to the Bethlehem's Fore River shipbuilding firm. The warring nations, however, signed an armistice on November 11, 1918, ending the war. Production at the shipyard ground to a halt, and Kennedy busied himself with trying to sell off surplus ships. By June 1919, Kennedy decided that the time had come for him to move on, and he secured a position with the Boston branch of the prestigious brokerage house of Hayden, Stone and Company. Though providing Kennedy with only half of his salary at the shipyards, the job at Hayden, Stone promised the ambitious young businessman a broader range of opportunities.

Galen Stone, one of the nation's most brilliant financial men, became Joe's mentor, teaching him the intricacies of the stock market and how to maneuver through corporate holdings to amass a vast personal fortune. In the early 1920s, before the federal government began regulating the stock market, a clever businessman could make millions by buying or selling stocks on the basis of inside information, important data not available to the general public. Among his many profitable acquisitions, Joe bought control of a chain of 31 New England movie theaters and soon thereafter acquired the regional franchise for Universal Pictures. By 1923, the wealthy father of five—Eunice had been born in 1921—quit Hayden, Stone and went out on his own as an independent capitalist.

Because Joe's business interests became centered on Wall Street in New York City, Rose and the children moved to the Riverdale section of the Bronx in 1926 to be closer to him. Kennedy continued to enjoy great success in the world of finance. For example, he engineered a brilliant behind-the-scenes stock maneuver in 1928 that helped halt the downturn in the price of Yellow Cab stock. As a result, Joe later admitted to *American Magazine*, "[s]everal of us emerged wealthy men."

In 1928, Rose and Joseph Kennedy, now the parents of eight children, return from a European tour aboard the S.S. Aquitania.

Meanwhile, Rose continued to attend to the growing household in Riverdale. By this time the family included Patricia, who was born in 1924, and Robert, who followed in 1925. Years later, Rose calculated that she gave birth to a child every 18 months after she and Joe got married.

Rose often commented that her "husband changed jobs so fast I simply never knew what business he was in." What she was sure of, however, was that no matter what industry Joe tackled, he always had to work long hours, leaving Rose to oversee the children and to cultivate their educational and religious values.

On rearing children, Rose stated in her autobiography that "you have to tend to the roots, as well as the stems, and slowly and carefully plant ideas and concepts of right and wrong, religion, social implication and applications." She cannot imagine a "greater aspiration and challenge for a mother than the hope of raising a great son or daughter." Even when the children were infants, Rose tried to take them to church every day so they would "form a habit of making God and religion a part of their daily lives."

Meanwhile, two more children joined the family. Jean was born in Riverdale in 1928, and in 1932, Edward, known as Teddy, was born in Bronxville, an affluent suburb in Westchester County, where the Kennedys had moved in 1928. Having to care for nine children forced Rose to be very organized. She established a system of note cards listing each child's height, weight, and illnesses. In her memoirs Rose described how "as each new baby came along, he or she was indexed and the card contained all the primary vital statistics." And when the children were little, Rose divided the front porch into cubicles so that they would have their own play area and not "knock each other down and gouge each other in the eyes with blunt toys."

Rose also developed her father's habit of pinning notes to himself to remember things. She rarely went anywhere without a notepad, even keeping one near her bed in case she thought of something one of the children might need the next day or some task one of the members of the hired help should tend to. Aside from managing the nursemaids and cooks and keeping track of each of the children's data, Rose focused on developing her children's character.

Along with sending them to the best schools and taking them to church regularly, Rose encouraged her children to exercise vigorously and to improve certain social graces, such as dancing.

The children took tennis lessons and played golf and were expected to play other competitive sports at school. Rose and Joe also advocated rivalry among the children themselves. Rose believed that "no matter what you did, you should try to be first."

To help her children with arithmetic, Rose often played one of her own childhood games, called Examples, with them. Rose would say, "Five times three, add one, divide by four, times eight, take away two, divide by three. What's the answer?" According to Rose, this game really helped her kids learn arithmetic. To instill a sense of competitiveness in her children at the same time, though,

Rose rehearsed a few Examples with Teddy, the youngest, and gave him the answers. When she recited those particular Examples in front of the rest of the children and Teddy jumped in with the answers almost immediately, the older children were amazed by Teddy's "ability" and worked hard to catch up to their little brother.

Rose drilled her children in table manners, deportment, and dress. She read to them constantly and listened to their nightly prayers. Rose also expected the children to discuss current events with her at dinner, which meant they had to read the newspaper every day. And she was always ready to provide informal history lessons. For example, if Rose and the children were walking past Boston's Old North Church, she made sure that they knew that in April 1775 the signal that the British were going to march on Lexington came from the church's steeple.

One unexpected cross Rose had to bear was her daughter Rosemary. When Rosemary was a toddler, it became apparent that she had been born with a mental disability. In her memoirs, Rose described how Rosemary "was slow in everything, and some things she seemed unable to learn how to do. When she was old enough for childish sports, for instance, I noticed that she couldn't steer her sled." Reading and writing were especially difficult for Rosemary.

Because of her learning disability, Rosemary could not recognize handwritten script letters of the alphabet. Rosemary was taught to use the printed forms so that words in a book would look like the words she tried to write. Rose changed her refined handwriting so that Rosemary would not think that her own handwriting was any different from her mother's.

Rose and Joe met with many experts in mental retardation from Harvard and other hospitals to discuss Rosemary's condition, but they were heartbroken at the lack of conclusive answers. The less progress Rosemary seemed to make, the more time Rose would spend helping her

Actress Gloria Swanson sails for Europe aboard the S.S. Berengaria *in 1924. Joseph Kennedy served as Swanson's financial adviser for many years, fueling persistent rumors that he enjoyed an adulterous relationship with the sultry screen star.*

along. The family treated Rosemary as normally as possible, trying not to indicate either within the family or outside that there was anything different about her. Knowing that Rosemary could not steer a sled well enough to get down the hill safely, Rose would arrange for the governess to take the other children sledding while she took Rosemary on a special walk to a nearby shopping center to look in department store windows. Eunice later recalled in Rose's memoirs that "Rosemary was never hidden away or anything, she was pushed right on with the rest of us."

Rose wanted Rosemary to feel accepted by her brothers and sisters and strongly encouraged the other children to include Rosemary in their activities. Eunice also remembered that at Rose's request she would take Rosemary swimming and sailing, and "Jack would take her to a dance at the club, and would dance with her and kid with her and would make sure a few of his close pals cut in, so she felt popular." Acting against most of the advice and social pressure that they received, Rose and Joe insisted on keeping Rosemary at home. Eunice remembers Joe asking psychologists, "What can they do in an institution that we can't do better for her at home here with her family?"

Although Joe's business activities were responsible for bringing the family to New York, Joe's additional investments in the movie business soon required him to travel to California frequently. Shortly after moving the family to New York, Joe acquired Film Booking Offices (FBO), an American film-producing company. In less than 3 years, FBO made more than 50 movies, mostly Westerns and melodramas that usually succeeded at the box office, if not with the critics. The Kennedy boys became the envy of neighborhood children in Bronxville when they received cowboy outfits from the movie sets.

In Hollywood, Kennedy competed with such movie moguls as Marcus Lowe, Louis B. Mayer, Samuel Goldwyn, Cecil B. deMille, and the four Warner brothers. One of his major projects in California was managing the career of the legendary film star Gloria Swanson. For a number of years, Kennedy served as Swanson's banker, intimate adviser, close friend, and frequent companion. As a producer of several of her films, Joe's close association with the sultry actress encouraged rumors of a lively romance. In her memoirs, Rose made no effort to ignore Swanson, but she implies a very professional, detached relationship.

In 1926, the Kennedys started taking summer vacations in Hyannis Port, Massachusetts, and bought a house there in 1928. Today Hyannis Port holds some of Rose's best memories because the whole family, including Joe, congregated there to go sailing, to play tennis and football, and to establish and maintain traditions that have continued to be enjoyed by the entire Kennedy clan.

At the West Beach Club in Hyannis Port, the children e ntered every available swimming competition, which usually saw six Kennedys in different age pairings competing. Although Rose did not enjoy sailing, the rest of the family sailed together as often as they could. And, of course, the children took every opportunity to play pranks on one another. Once, the boys left Kathleen stranded on a rock and did not come back for two hours. Rose was furious, and warned all the girls from then on, "Now, be careful dear," before they left to play with the boys.

In the meantime, Joe continued to take advantage of the soaring stock market in the late 1920s. With his associates, Joe took over the Keith-Albee-Orpheum theater chain and orchestrated a $500,000 merger with David Sarnoff of RCA. Joe accurately anticipated the catastrophic stock market collapse of 1929, turning potential disaster into personal profit. He liquidated most of his personal stock portfolio before the bottom fell out of the market and established a sizable trust fund for his children.

When Kennedy pulled out of the movie business in the early 1930s, he turned his attention to politics. Although he never ran for elective office, Kennedy provided sub-

The Kennedys purchased this spacious summer home in Hyannis Port, Massachusetts, in 1928. The Kennedy compound, as the estate became known, has served as the hub of the family's life ever since.

stantial financial assistance to Franklin Delano Roosevelt in his 1932 presidential campaign. In her memoirs, Rose described Joe as "one of the earliest, most ardent, and most effective of Roosevelt's supporters." Kennedy knew the country's most influential financiers and how to talk to them in ways they would understand and respect. Joe convinced many of them, including William Randolph Hearst, the powerful publisher, to support Roosevelt's New Deal—a package of legislative reforms designed to turn the nation back toward economic prosperity.

In exchange for his support, Kennedy expected to be appointed to an important cabinet position in the new administration. Although Kennedy let it be known that he was very interested in becoming the secretary of the Treasury, Roosevelt delayed naming him to any post. Finally, two years after the election, the president nominated Kennedy to the chairmanship of the Securities and Exchange Commission (SEC), which Congress established to regu-

In 1934, eight of the Kennedy children surround their parents: (foreground, left to right) Patricia, Edward, Rosemary, Eunice, and Kathleen; (standing, left to right), John, Jean, and Robert. Joe, Jr., is not pictured.

On February 18, 1938, Joseph Kennedy (left) takes the oath as the new U.S. ambassador to the United Kingdom from Chief Justice Stanley Reed as President Franklin Roosevelt looks on. Kennedy had previously served in the Roosevelt adminstration as chairman of the U.S. Maritime Commission and as chairman of the Securities and Exchange Commission.

late the trading of stocks, bonds, and other securities to protect investors from fraud.

Because Joe planned on serving as chairman of the SEC in Washington, D.C., for only about a year, he and Rose decided not to move the family there. Although Kennedy did resign the chairmanship of the SEC a little more than a year later, he helped establish an agency that is regarded as one of the most important achievements of Roosevelt's administration. The SEC helped restore confidence in the securities markets, which had continued to struggle after the stock market crash in 1929, by ensuring that corporations issuing securities—and brokers trading them—dealt honestly with the public.

After his landslide victory in the 1936 presidential election, Roosevelt appointed Kennedy chairman of the U.S. Maritime Commission. His job was to revitalize the nation's merchant shipping industry, an assignment Joe often referred to as his most difficult. It involved complex mediation between labor unions and employer groups. A year later, after Robert Worth Bingham, the U.S. ambassador to the United Kingdom, resigned his post, Roosevelt chose Kennedy to replace Bingham. All of the Kennedys—

In March 1938, Rose and Joseph Kennedy prepare to leave their London home to attend a gala performance at London's Covent Garden. As the wife of the U.S. ambassador, Rose served as the hostess of many official dinners and parties at the U.S. embassy.

5

The Court of St. James's

"THIS IS A HELLUVA LONG WAY FROM EAST BOSTON," Joe said to Rose after looking around the opulent suite of rooms in Windsor Castle, where the newly appointed ambassador and his wife would spend a weekend visit with the king and queen of England. The Kennedys came to Windsor Castle for a weekend in April 1938 shortly after Joe assumed his post as the Ambassador to the Court of St. James's, the official title of the U.S. ambassador to the United Kingdom. British prime minister Neville Chamberlain and his wife, the foreign secretary Lord Halifax and his wife Lady Halifax, and the queen's sister, Lady Elphinstone, and her husband Lord Elphinstone joined the Kennedys for the weekend at Windsor Castle.

After settling into their guest quarters, Joe and Rose were escorted to a large receiving room. Once all the visitors assembled, King George VI and Queen Elizabeth entered to greet their company. At dinner, Rose sat beside King George, who spoke to her at length about the Kennedy children. While lying in bed that night, Rose recalled in her memoirs thinking to herself, "I must be dreaming that I, Rose Kennedy, a simple, young matron from Boston, am really here at Windsor Castle." In a year filled with glamorous social events attended by heads of state, dignitaries, and royalty, that April weekend remained one of the most fascinating events of Rose's life.

In addition to her exciting new social life, Rose had other reasons to relish the time that she spent in London. She was proud to be the wife of the first Irish-American U.S. ambassador to England, and she was happy to have all nine of her children together again. During the nine years preceding Kennedy's appointment as ambassador, the family had only rarely been together. Rose's husband was often away from home looking after his business

Joined by five of their children, Joseph and Rose Kennedy confidently stride down a London street. The charm and vitality of the ambassador's large Irish-American family captivated the English people.

interests or working at the SEC or the Maritime Commission in Washington, D.C. Her oldest son, Joe, Jr., had entered Choate, an elite prep school in Connecticut. Rose continued to live in the Kennedy's Bronxville home while some of the other children attended boarding school.

The large, boisterous Kennedy clan took London by storm. Joe, Jr., and John worked for their father at the embassy, and the younger children attended school in or near London. In her memoirs, Rose described the years in England as "by far the happiest years of my married life." The Kennedys lived in a palatial 36-room mansion in the fashionable Knightsbridge section of London. Rose and Joe maintained a busy social schedule that required their appearance at major events. The two Irish Americans from East Boston radiated charm and panache as they mingled with English royalty.

For Rose, the calendar of events, parties, elegant dinners, and weekends—and the fancy clothes that she required for them—filled her days with excitement. Not since she was the mayor's daughter and hostess had Rose enjoyed such attention and prominence. Kennedy relied on his wife to be the hostess of the affairs held at the embassy. Rose knew when to speak about politics and when to keep the conversation on children and other less sensitive subjects. She never let down her guard.

Young Teddy and Bobby were fascinated by their new world—from the elevator in the embassy building to the swans in Hyde Park, which stretched out across the street. Of the five girls, Kathleen especially enjoyed London. The 18-year-old Kick, as she was called, proved instantly popular with the fashionable crowd of young English gentlemen. She had a bubbly personality that everyone loved. According to Doris Goodwin, "The British had seldom seen a girl with such vitality and informality, so brash, so outspoken and so obviously American." Goodwin also records that Lady Astor's niece, Dinah Bridge, said of Kick, "When she came into a room, everybody

Dressed in their finest formal ball gowns, Kathleen, Rosemary, and Rose Kennedy prepare to leave for Buckingham Palace, where they will be presented to the king and queen of England at the first court of the 1938 social season.

seemed to lighten up; she makes everyone feel terribly happy and gay."

However idyllic these years were for the Kennedy family, the political tensions building in Europe would prove too much for Joe to navigate as the highest-ranking U.S. diplomat in the United Kingdom. The threat of war loomed large over Europe as Adolf Hitler, Germany's head of state, aggressively pursued annexations of German-speaking Austria and the Sudetenland, a region of Czechoslovakia where many ethnic Germans lived. The rise of Hitler's Third Reich deeply troubled the United Kingdom and France. But the horrifying experience of World War I, with its suffering and enormous loss of life, made world leaders—British prime minister Chamberlain foremost among them—anxious to avoid another war at almost any political cost.

Kennedy, who firmly believed that wars caused great economic harm and ultimately solved nothing, agreed that armed conflict should be circumvented through diplomacy. During the April weekend that the Kennedys spent with the royal family at Windsor Castle, Joe voiced the views that most Americans held at the time. He told Queen Elizabeth, "What the American people fear more than anything else is being involved in a war. When they remember 1917 and how they went in to make the world safe for democracy and then they look now at the crop of dictatorships, quarrels and miseries arising out of that war they say to themselves, 'Never again!' And I can't say I blame them. I feel the same way myself."

During a long conversation with Chamberlain that same weekend, Kennedy listened to the prime minister's characterization of Hitler. Kennedy asserted, "It seems to me that the big question is whether Hitler means to limit his activities to helping his Germans or whether he has further objectives that will violate the self-determination of other nations." Chamberlain concurred: "Yet the only way we can find the answer is to wait and see. Up to now every one of Hitler's demands has concerned Germans and he undoubtedly has a majority of his people behind him." Chamberlain went on to note Hitler's statements about Germany's future expansion to the east. But the prime minister said, "If he means economic penetration without force, we cannot very well object. Besides, war wins nothing, ends nothing. In a modern war there are no victors." Chamberlain believed that pacification—acceding to some of Hitler's territorial demands in order to avoid war—was to every nation's advantage.

But as the historical drama in Europe unfolded in 1938 and 1939, the wisdom of this policy of appeasement, which Chamberlain and Kennedy wholeheartedly supported, proved unsound. Some world leaders disagreed with Chamberlain's position. Among the most prominent, and certainly the most charismatic, was Winston Churchill, an outspoken member of England's Parliament. Following negotiations in Munich in the fall of 1938 that conceded to Hitler his demand for Germany's annexation of the Sudentenland, Churchill declared, "Our brave people should know that we have sustained a defeat without a war." While the English people rejoiced in the news that war had been averted, Churchill maintained his almost solitary voice of opposition. "This is only the first sip," he said at the time, "the first foretaste of a bitter cup which will be proffered to us year by year unless, by a supreme recovery of moral health and market vigor, we arise again and take our stand for freedom."

Kennedy felt in his heart that war, the ultimate consequence of Churchill's stance, would bring down civilization as he had known it. Commerce between the United States and Europe would grind to a halt. With Europe in ruins, the ambassador must have thought, communism could gain control. Now 50 years old, Joe feared that the enormous wealth he had amassed would be irretrievably lost in a war. In a conversation with former secretary of state Henry L. Stimson in July 1938, Kennedy told Stimson

Flanked by two of the Vatican's Swiss Guards, the members of the Kennedy family await their audience with Pope Pius XII in 1939. The Kennedys had attended the pope's coronation on the previous day.

that he lay awake at night worrying that all of his hard work to provide for the financial security of his children would prove useless. He also worried that Joe, Jr., age 23, and John, age 21, might be drafted and killed in action.

While the political situation in Europe rapidly deteriorated in the spring of 1939, Kennedy was appointed the official U.S. representative at the coronation of Eugenio Cardinal Pacelli as Pope Pius XII. It was the first time a U.S. president had sent an official representative to such an occasion. The entire Kennedy family, except for Joe, Jr., who was in Madrid at the time, made the trip to Rome. Rose was especially honored to attend the coronation because, many years earlier, Cardinal Pacelli had come to the Kennedy home when he visited New York City. The day after the coronation, the new pope received the Kennedy family in his private quarters and presented the children with rosaries that he had blessed. Rose never forgot the experience. During Pius XII's 19-year reign, he named only one papal countess—Rose Kennedy.

Back in London, Kennedy's unwavering support of Chamberlain began to become a political liability. By linking his diplomatic status to Chamberlain's policies, Kennedy risked a confrontation with Roosevelt, who privately thought that the Munich agreement might lead to disaster. Despite his personal affection for Kennedy, Roosevelt slowly began to distance the United States's official position from that of its ambassador to England, whose duty was to represent the views of his government rather than his own.

The conflicting opinions of Roosevelt and Kennedy collided head-on when the ambassador delivered a speech reiterating his isolationist views and supporting Chamberlain's policy of appeasement. Three weeks earlier, Chamberlain had returned from Munich, proclaiming that his agreement with Hitler had brought "peace in our time." Churchill condemned the agreement: "Britain and France had to choose between war and dishonor. They chose dishonor. They will have war." Within the three weeks between Chamberlain's return from Munich and Kennedy's speech, world opinion had turned from complete support for Chamberlain and the Munich agreement to utter distaste for what many perceived to be the international community's betrayal of the people of Czechoslovakia.

In his imprudent speech, Kennedy called upon both camps to work together to solve common problems. As soon as Kennedy had finished his address, telegrams questioning and criticizing the ambassador's remarks flooded the White House and the State Department. Had U.S. policy, which Roosevelt had carefully outlined a year earlier, changed? Did the United States plan to befriend so great a foe to freedom and democracy as Hitler's Germany?

Forced to affirm that there had been no change in U.S. policy, Roosevelt delivered a radio address that repudiated Kennedy's speech. From that moment on, the strong friendship between the two men began to unravel. Meanwhile, Hitler let nobody mistake his intentions. In March 1939, he ordered German forces to occupy Prague, Czechoslovakia, marking the Third Reich's first invasion of non-German-speaking lands. At that point, Chamberlain pledged England's support to Poland should Hitler have designs on that nation. After a tense summer, German armored divisions rolled into Poland on September 1, 1939. The United Kingdom declared war on Germany the following day.

Joe, Jr., Jack, and Kick went to the House of Commons to witness the historic debate over the declaration of war. The next day, Rose and the rest of the family prepared to take a ship back to the United States. But Joe remained at his post in London to gather information for the State Department. Under the incredible pressures brought about by the impending conflict, he lost 15 pounds in the weeks that followed the United Kingdom's declaration of war. Kennedy grew increasingly upset with the treatment he was receiving from the State Department. He felt that he was being excluded from important decisions and projects, such as the deal Roosevelt struck with Churchill to lend U.S. ships to the Royal Navy. Kennedy continued to speak out against U.S. involvement in the war, even as the countries of Scandinavia and then France fell to the German onslaught in the spring of 1940.

From airfields in France, the Luftwaffe, the German air force, began launching bombing raids that strafed southeastern England and then London itself in August 1940. Despite the danger, Kennedy remained at his post. He was amazed and impressed by the resilience and high spirits of the English during the intense bombardments.

On September 1, 1939, Kathleen Kennedy and her two brothers, Joe, Jr. (left), and John (right), arrive at Westminster Palace to watch the House of Commons deliberate whether or not England should declare war against Germany.

When it appeared that the Royal Air Force had fought the Luftwaffe to a draw, Kennedy asked President Roosevelt for permission to return to the United States. A year had passed since Rose and the children had left London. Joe visited the royal family and other dignitaries to say farewell before he departed. He also called on his friend Neville Chamberlain, who had recently been defeated in a vote of confidence in the House of Commons and had stepped aside to allow Churchill to become prime minister.

Kennedy intended to resign his position as ambassador because he was so upset with what he perceived as mistreatment by Roosevelt's administration. The 1940 presidential election was a month away at this time, and Roosevelt wanted Kennedy's public endorsement for his unprecedented campaign for a third term in office. The

In September 1939, Kathleen, Bobby, Eunice, and Rose Kennedy arrive in New York from London aboard the S.S. Washington. *The ship was jammed with Americans fleeing Europe in the wake of England's declaration of war against Germany.*

In a radio address on October 29, 1940, Joseph Kennedy delivers an emphatic endorsement for President Franklin D. Roosevelt, who was seeking an unprecedented third term in office. Following Roosevelt's victory in the November election, Kennedy resigned as ambassador and returned to private life.

president apologized for the treatment Kennedy had received and asked him to give a speech to support his candidacy.

Kennedy gave a convincing radio address that spoke strongly of Roosevelt's opposition to U.S. involvement in the war. Some said it was the most resounding endorsement Roosevelt had received from anyone. In closing his speech, Kennedy declared, "My wife and I have given nine hostages to fortune. Our children and your children are more important than anything else in the world. The kind of America that they and their children will inherit is of grave concern to us all. In the light of these considerations, I believe that Franklin D. Roosevelt should be re-elected President of the United States." After Roosevelt defeated the Republican candidate, Wendell Willkie, Joe tendered his resignation. He was satisfied that he had repaid everything that he owed to his friend, who after all had named him to three important positions in the U.S. government.

During the early years of the European war, the Kennedy family remained active on several fronts. Joe, Jr., served as a Massachusetts delegate to the Democratic National Convention in 1940. John wrote a senior thesis at Harvard entitled "Appeasement at Munich," which explored the United Kingdom's lack of preparation for confronting the German threat and the failure of the policy of pacification. The thesis was published in book form in 1940 under the title *Why England Slept*.

As the prospect of U.S. involvement in the war grew, the demands on the family mounted as well. Joe, Jr., interrupted his studies at Harvard Law School after two years to join the U.S. Navy. He trained to be a pilot, which

Joseph Kennedy, Jr., poses beside an airplane at a military base in Squantum, Massachusetts, where he began aviation training in July 1941. His brother, John, once remarked, "Joe was the star of the family. He did everything better than the rest of us."

was considered to be the most difficult and most dangerous military assignment. John, despite being rejected by the military several times because of his poor health, finally enlisted in the navy in 1941. He was given a job with Naval Intelligence in Washington, D.C., where he prepared reports using information sent by intelligence sources abroad.

John later received an assignment as commander of a patrol torpedo (PT) boat in the South Pacific. In August 1943, his boat sank after colliding with a Japanese destroyer in Blackett Strait in the Solomon Islands. John's heroic actions saved the lives of 10 crew members of PT-109. On August 6, 1943, Rose was listening intently to war news on the radio when she heard an announcement that Lieutenant John F. Kennedy had been saved. Rose had no idea that her son was missing in action; Joe had been informed of John's status four days earlier but was so upset that he was unable to tell the family, not even his wife.

Adding to Rose's anxiety, Kick volunteered—against her mother's wishes—to work for the Red Cross in England in May 1943. Billy Cavendish, a young English nobleman, resumed his courtship of Kathleen, which had been interrupted when Kick had returned to the United States after the war broke out in September 1939.

On May 6, 1944, Kick and Billy were married. Rose strongly opposed her daughter's marriage to a Protestant whose ancestors had occupied the highest offices in the English government of Ireland. Rose claimed in her memoirs that "they had done their best to suppress any sentiments for independence among or on behalf of the Irish." The only family member present at Kick's wedding in London was Joe, Jr., who was serving in England at the time. When Cavendish was called up to fight with British troops three weeks after the marriage, Kick returned to Massachusetts to visit her family. Despite her feelings about Kick and Billy, Rose welcomed her daughter back home.

Kathleen Kennedy Cavendish and her husband, William, emerge from the church after their 1944 wedding. Joe, Jr., the only member of the Kennedy family to attend the wedding, stands behind the happy couple.

As the war moved toward its conclusion in the summer of 1944, Joe, Jr., serving as a pilot in England, received his orders to return to the United States. However, he volunteered for a dangerous secret bombing mission. On August 12, 1944, Kennedy's plane, laden with tons of high explosives, exploded as it began to cross the English Channel en route to its target.

The death of their oldest son was a terrible blow to Rose and Joe. Joe, Jr., had so much vitality, intelligence, and social grace. As Rose described in her memoirs, she and Joe decided to find "a way to turn some part of the loss to a positive, affirmative use for the benefit of other people." Choosing to work toward improving the plight of the mentally retarded, they established the Joseph P. Kennedy, Jr., Foundation. The foundation has donated millions of dollars to hospitals, institutions, day-care centers, and research projects benefiting the mentally retarded.

With her daughter Eunice and her son John looking on, Rose Kennedy speaks at a formal tea during John's 1952 campaign for the U.S. Senate. Over the years, she has contributed considerable time and energy to the campaigns of her sons John, Robert, and Edward.

6

The Mother
of the President

JOE, JR.'S, LOFTY AMBITION to become the first Irish-Catholic president of the United States passed to his younger brother, John. When John was discharged from the navy in the spring of 1945, he worked briefly as a special correspondent for the Hearst newspapers. But as Rose explained in her memoirs, later that year, the "combination of time, place, and circumstance made the idea of Jack running for Congress attractive and reasonable." James Michael Curley, U.S. congressman for the Eleventh District, was elected mayor of Boston in 1945 and vacated his seat. Although the boundaries had been slightly redrawn, the Eleventh District was basically the same district that John's grandfather, John Francis Fitzgerald, had represented 50 years earlier.

John—a bright and wealthy young war hero who was already associated in the mind of the public with selflessness, patriotism, and public service—had firsthand knowledge of politics from his grandfather, his father, and his mother.

And Johnny, Joe, and Rose all played major roles in the young Kennedy's first campaign. Although John was virtually unknown in

In October 1950, Rose Kennedy joins Francis Cardinal Spellman at ceremonies dedicating the Joseph P. Kennedy, Jr., Home for Children in New York City. In honor of their deceased son, the Kennedys established the Joseph P. Kennedy, Jr., Foundation, a charity committed to helping mentally retarded people.

the Eleventh District, no one had forgotten his grandfather. Honey Fitz returned to the North End with his grandson, introducing him to his old friends at City Hall. Because Kennedy faced 10 opponents in the Democratic primary, he had to make himself known to the people in the district.

While John walked throughout the district to meet voters, his father worked behind the scenes from a suite in the Ritz Carlton Hotel. Joe called everyone he knew who could help his son's campaign and who might owe the elder Kennedy a favor. Recognizing the power of the press to influence public opinion, Joe immediately began to enlist local newspapers as allies. The *Boston American* assigned a full-time reporter to the Kennedy headquarters but not to those of the other candidates. It has also been rumored that Joe spent $250,000 on John's campaign— a staggering amount for a congressional campaign in the 1940s.

But according to Dave Powers, one of Joe's closest associates and confidants, it was Rose who was John's greatest asset. She understood precinct politics in Boston better than anyone on her son's campaign committee. She knew that success depended on the candidate projecting charisma, on knowing more people in the precincts than his opponents, and never forgetting their names. According to Powers, she had "uncanny knowledge of the innumerable little details of campaigning in Boston."

While campaigning for her son, Rose never attended parties held in private homes; they were too intimate, too informal for her. Rose always maintained an air of royalty, which worked to her advantage. Bostonians were fascinated by this woman who was so close to the local and international political leaders whom they had known throughout the years.

The crowning achievement of Rose's efforts in John's first campaign for Congress came when she hosted a tea party at the Hotel Commodore in Cambridge. Kennedy campaign workers sent out 2,000 hand-addressed invitations, mostly to women whom they thought would want to meet Rose Kennedy and her remarkable family. The tea party served to bring voters in contact with the candidate. The invitees felt more important having met John and Rose personally, and they were sure to tell all their friends about the experience.

John campaigned hard day and night to win the primary. When the votes were tallied, Kennedy captured more than 40 percent of the vote. He went on to win the congressional election in a landslide over his Republican opponent. Kennedy was easily reelected in 1948 and again in 1950. Although Rose did not have to actively participate in her son's reelection campaigns, she went back on the campaign trail when he ran for the U.S. Senate in 1952.

Before John's campaign for the U.S. Senate, however, Rose mourned the deaths of one of her daughters and her father. On May 13, 1948, Kathleen died in an airplane crash while flying from London to Cannes, France. Kathleen had remained in England despite the death of her husband, Billy, who had been killed in action during the last days of the war. She had built a full life for herself in England, and the family had not seen her for several years. Kathleen had arranged to see her father, who planned to be in Paris on business, to announce her engagement to Lord Peter Fitzwilliam, a wealthy English nobleman.

The couple decided to spend two days on the French Riviera before the meeting with Joe. After a refueling stop

On June 17, 1946, John Kennedy votes with his grandparents Josephine and John Fitzgerald in the Massachusetts primary. Kennedy won the primary and then defeated his Republican opponent in the November general election to secure a seat in the U.S. House of Representatives.

in Paris, their small chartered airplane encountered a violent thunderstorm and crashed into a mountain peak in the south of France, instantly killing everyone on board. Joe identified his 28-year-old daughter's body after he watched rescue crews bring it down from the cliffs. Rose flew to Derbyshire, England, to be with Joe for the funeral of her beloved daughter.

On October 2, 1950, Rose's father, Johnny, died at the age of 87 in his suite at the Bellevue Hotel in Boston. Rose, who was vacationing in Paris at the time, immediately returned to Boston for the funeral. She was devastated. After Johnny's death, Rose said, "In spite of his age, it was impossible to conceive of life without him." Rose also wished her father had lived long enough to witness the 1952 Senate race between John and Henry Cabot Lodge II, the grandson of the man who had defeated Johnny in a Senate race 36 years earlier.

Securing a Senate seat was a logical stepping-stone in Kennedy's political career. It would give him more of a national platform and better credentials for dealing with foreign affairs, opening a possible route for the presidency. The expiration of Senator Henry Cabot Lodge II's term in 1952 offered John an enticing opportunity. Pollsters working for Joe Kennedy determined that his son would have a better chance of defeating Lodge than of defeating Leverett Saltonstall, the senior Republican senator from Massachusetts. Joe worked full-time on John's campaign, renting an apartment in downtown Boston so that he could be closer to the action. The rest of the family also devoted themselves to the campaign. Bobby Kennedy, who had just graduated from law school, was brought in as his brother's campaign manager. Rose and her daughters worked tirelessly to secure the women's vote.

In *Front Runner, Dark Horse* (1960), journalists Ralph Martin and Ed Plaut described Rose's role in the 1952 senatorial campaign:

Mrs. Kennedy knew exactly what to say, what to wear, what to do, no matter what the audience. A *New York Times* reporter followed and watched and said, "Mrs. Kennedy carefully selected her accessories and tailored her remarks. Thus to a group of Italian women in the North End, she was the mother of nine children, one of whom died in the war. Perhaps a single pearl necklace over a black dress would be worn. Before a Chestnut Hill group of matrons, she might don a mink stole and a few rings and certainly a different hat." In the cars between appearances, she would put on jewelry or strip it off to fit the occasion, appearing as the daughter of Honey Fitz to one crowd and the wife of the former ambassador to the Court of St. James's to another crowd.

Rose also attended 30 formal teas throughout Massachusetts, much like the tea party that she hosted during Jack's campaign in 1946. The announcements for the teas read, "Reception in honor of Mrs. Joseph P. Kennedy, and her son, Congressman John F. Kennedy." At the gatherings, John would tell the women how much he needed their votes, and he would insist that his grandfather Johnny lost to Henry Cabot Lodge I because women did not yet have the right to vote in 1916. John's aunt Polly Fitzgerald, who organized the teas, later told Gail Cameron that "Mrs. Kennedy was the big drawing card." Then 62 years old, Rose was vivacious and always immaculately dressed.

According to Cameron, "[t]he Kennedys were so glamorous and so exciting that it became a status symbol to support them." Rose's younger children twice appeared on a television show called "Coffee with the Kennedys." Everywhere the Kennedys went, they were greeted with keen interest and awe.

In contrast to Kennedy, who spent every waking moment trying to attract votes, Lodge was confident that he would win reelection to the Senate. He spent a considerable amount of time outside Massachusetts campaigning for Dwight D. Eisenhower, the Republican candidate for

In May 1953, Rose Kennedy arrives at St. Patrick's Cathedral in New York City for the marriage of her daughter Eunice to Sargent Shriver. Robert, John, Patricia, Jean, and Edward were also married during the 1950s.

president. The hard work of the Kennedy clan paid off; Jack upset Lodge by more than 70,000 votes. When Rose heard the news of the decisive victory, she exclaimed, "At last the Fitzgeralds have evened the score with the Lodges."

During the 1950s, all of Rose's surviving children except Rosemary married. Bobby was the first, marrying Ethel Skakel in 1950. In 1953, Eunice married Robert

Rose Kennedy holds a bouquet of red roses that were presented to her when she arrived in Columbus, Ohio, to speak on behalf of her son John during the 1960 presidential campaign.

Sargent Shriver, a businessman who worked for Joe Kennedy. That same year, John—who had often been called the nation's most eligible bachelor—married Jacqueline Bouvier, a beautiful and intelligent photojournalist. In 1954, Patricia married actor Peter Lawford, and one year later Jean married Stephen Smith, a New York City businessman. Teddy married Joan Bennett in 1957. "It was as if Jack's marriage opened the door for the rest," Rose observed in her memoirs, "for within the next few years they all seemed to follow each other down the aisle."

On January 20, 1960, John Kennedy announced his candidacy for the presidency. Early in that year, Rose traveled to New Hampshire and Wisconsin to campaign for her son in the primaries. She appeared at several gatherings each day, delivering speeches before college groups and women's clubs and giving television interviews.

Gail Cameron noted that there was "never a question, however blunt and even intimidating, that she could not turn to a political advantage." For example, Rose repeatedly defended John's youth, claiming that younger people have "a great deal of vigor, enthusiasm, and idealism, which we need now." In response to criticism about John's seemingly overzealous quest for power, Rose simply stated the obvious: "If you're in politics, I suppose you always work to get to the top." Furthermore, Rose assured people that John would not lead them into war because "his oldest brother had died in the war, so Jack knows the sorrow, the grief, the tears, and the heart-breaking grief and loneliness that comes when a mother has lost her eldest son." Rose always knew the right thing to say.

In July 1960, the Kennedys traveled to the Democratic National Convention in Los Angeles, California. Because of his success in the primaries, John easily won the party's nomination on the first ballot. Rose recalled in her memoirs that "[t]here was joyful, ear-shattering pandemonium." She and the rest of the Kennedys joined John on the platform as the delegates cheered and waved placards and flags.

The race between Kennedy and the Republican candidate, Vice-president Richard M. Nixon, was close right up to the end. On November 8, family members and friends assembled at the Kennedy compound in Hyannis Port to watch the election returns. They were thrilled when the early returns gave Jack a lead over Nixon. But by midnight the race tightened considerably. At 4:00 A.M., the votes in California and Illinois remained to be counted. The results in those two states could put either candidate over the top. The family speculated that Nixon would win his home state, California, which meant that John had to win Illinois. By 6:00 A.M., Joe's informants in Illinois notified him that John had prevailed in that state. Other smaller states followed suit, and by 9:00 A.M. the outcome was clear: John F. Kennedy had won the presidency.

Later that morning, Rose and the family drove to the Hyannis Port Armory, where news cameras and reporters were waiting. On the platform, Rose proudly sat next to her son and held her chin high in triumph. In the heady days that followed, Jack named his cabinet. He took the best and brightest of his generation. For example, he chose Robert McNamara, former president of Ford Motor Company, to head the Defense Department and McGeorge Bundy, a 41-year-old Harvard professor, as one of his top foreign policy advisers. The new president did not look far for someone to oversee the Department of Justice, appointing his brother Bobby as attorney general. Bobby became one of Jack's closest advisers.

Kennedy's tenure in office was marked by the continuation of the cold war, the period of intense mutual distrust between the United States and the Soviet Union that lasted from about 1945 to 1963. These two countries, which had emerged from World War II as the strongest nations in the world, were at the time the only nations with nuclear weapons capable of mass destruction. Each superpower sought opportunities to expand their influence in the world at the expense of the other.

One of Kennedy's crowning moments of international acclaim came when he spoke in West Berlin, a city cut off from Western Europe by its geographic position inside Communist East Germany. To the throngs that listened to his speech, he represented the future of freedom and democracy. They cheered Kennedy when he declared, *"Ich bin auch ein Berliner,"* (I, too, am a Berliner) reassuring them of the United States's moral and political support for the freedom of their city.

Confrontations with the Soviet Union also occurred perilously close to home. Following the public humiliation of the Bay of Pigs incident—a failed attempt by the Central Intelligence Agency (CIA) in April 1961 to topple Fidel Castro from power in Cuba—Kennedy displayed decisive leadership during the Cuban Missile Crisis. In October 1962, aerial reconnaissance revealed that the Soviet Union intended to place offensive nuclear missiles in Cuba, which would threaten the nations of the Western Hemisphere. Kennedy successfully stopped the deployment of Soviet missiles by ordering U.S. warships to surround Cuba, establishing a blockade to intercept any Soviet ships that were carrying missiles. After five tense days during which nuclear war seemed inevitable, the Soviet Union agreed to withdraw their missiles in exchange for U.S. assurances that it would not invade Cuba.

During these years, Rose enjoyed the attention of a world that admired her son. She was a special guest wherever she went, and Rose traveled frequently. She loved to go to Paris, where she would take French lessons and buy the latest fashions. From Paris, Rose traveled around the rest of Europe. Everywhere she went, she met famous personalities, such as ambassadors and heads of state, and she enjoyed a special stature as the "queen mother of Camelot." (Some people had compared Kennedy's administration with Camelot, the court of King Arthur, the legendary Celtic king.)

At the family's home in Hyannis Port, the Kennedys enjoy a casual moment soon after John's victory in the presidential election.

On November 20, 1969, Senator Edward Kennedy escorts his mother from St. Francis Xavier Church in Hyannis, Massachusetts, following the funeral service for Joseph Kennedy, Sr. The death of the Kennedy patriarch culminated a decade of recurrent tragedies for the family.

7

❁

A Turbulent Decade

THE ENCHANTED LIFE OF THE KENNEDY FAMILY began to disintegrate when the first of a series of tragedies struck on the morning of December 16, 1961. As Joe Kennedy prepared to tee off on the 10th hole at the Palm Beach Country Club golf course, he began to feel faint. Blaming his uneasiness on a cold that had bothered him for a few days, the 73-year-old Kennedy continued to play. On the 16th hole, he again felt dizzy and had to sit down. Ann Gargan, Rose's niece, was Joe's golf partner that day. She escorted him off the course and drove him to the Kennedys' summer house on North Ocean Boulevard. On his way to his bedroom to rest, Kennedy suffered a massive stroke and was rushed to St. Mary's Hospital.

Rose was away from the house when her husband was stricken. After morning mass, she had done some Christmas shopping, not returning home until almost noon. Rose rushed to the hospital upon hearing the news. She later recalled spending "most of the time in the hospital chapel, praying, praying." The stroke had left Kennedy unable to speak and with almost complete paralysis of his right arm and leg. "His mind, however," Rose described in her memoirs, "had been only moderately impaired."

Although Kennedy was able to walk for a while with a cane, he spent most of his time confined to bed and a wheelchair. With the help of Ann Gargan and a staff of nurses, Kennedy worked hard at rehabilitation, but his condition only deteriorated over the next seven years. Gargan devoted herself to caring for Joe. After Agnes Fitzgerald Gargan died suddenly in 1936, Rose and Joe Kennedy had become almost second parents to her children, Ann, Mary Jo, and Joseph. As the Gargan children grew older, they began to spend summers and holidays with the Kennedys, and as Rose explained in her memoirs, "[I]n a real sense, they became members of our own family." Ann rarely left Joe's side after he suffered his stroke.

For probably the first time in his life, Joe Kennedy was dependent on other people. One of the few diary notes that Rose took soon after Joe's illness expresses the heartache that she felt over her husband's condition: "The grief when I see him cry and the pity when I see one who was so strong and independent lie helpless in bed, saying 'no, no, no.' Sometimes when he means, 'yes.'"

Rose Kennedy and Joan Bennett Kennedy leave the Senate Gallery after watching Edward Kennedy, Rose's son and Joan's husband, sworn in as a U.S. senator in January 1963.

Because of what Rose described as her husband's "tremendous determination," Joe continued to take part in some of his former activities. He went into his New York office every few weeks for about an hour or two at a time, and he and Rose even traveled to Washington, D.C., to spend a few days in the White House with John and Jackie. Rose notes that whenever Joe was at the White House, "Jack made sure to be with him several times a day, give him the news of government and, in the most respectful and tactful way, solicit his advice, so far as he could give it." Rose was proud of her children's sensitivity to Joe after his stroke.

Later the next year, Teddy ran for the U.S. Senate from Massachusetts and won, giving Rose another reason to be proud. "As soon as he could be certain of his victory," Rose wrote in her memoirs, "Teddy called his father. Joe couldn't speak, but he listened as Ted told him the news and all that he knew his father would want to know."

"When Teddy was elected," Rose noted in a rare self-praising moment, "when all 3 of our surviving sons were in positions of leadership, then I—looking back over all the years to when they had been children, little boys on their way to youth and manhood, those impressionable years when 'the twig is bent'—thought to myself that I must have done something right."

On November 22, 1963, however, the Kennedy family's life turned upside down. Rose and Joe were in Hyannis Port enjoying the peace and tranquillity of Cape Cod after the summer tourists had gone. They were eagerly looking forward to their children arriving for the family's traditional Thanksgiving weekend.

The day began like any other for Rose. As usual, she attended morning mass at St. Francis Xavier on South Street in Hyannis, lingering afterward for private meditation. And then, after having breakfast with Joe, Rose played nine holes of golf at the Hyannisport Club, carrying her own clubs in a canvas golf bag.

During her customary afternoon nap, however, Rose was awakened by the sound of a blaring television, which her niece Ann and her maid Dora were watching in a state of shocked disbelief. As the breaking story unfolded before her eyes, Rose trembled, fearing the worst.

Shortly after arriving in Dallas for an official visit, John and Jackie joined Texas governor John Connally and his wife for a drive through the downtown section of the city. As the motorcade entered Dealey Plaza, an assassin, Lee Harvey Oswald, fired three shots at the governor's limousine from the sixth-floor window of the Texas School Book Depository building. The first bullet struck Kennedy in the throat; the second shattered his skull. Governor Connally was hit in the back. Soon after arriving at Parkland Hospital, the 46-year-old president died. Within a few hours, outrage and overwhelming grief swept the nation and the world.

Rose was overcome with the need to "keep moving." She explained in her memoirs how her grief took the form of nervous energy. She kept "moving, walking, praying to [herself]." Even as the afternoon air turned chilly, Rose continued to pace up and down the beach. Rose noted in her memoirs that she probably put on the same old warm coat she had worn when she trudged through the snow to get to mass the morning of John's inauguration.

Rose insisted that Ann and the household staff not tell Joe about John's death until the next morning, when Teddy and her other children would be there. Bobby flew to Dallas to be with Jackie. Ann later told Gail Cameron that Rose was terribly worried what the news would do to Joe. "If anything happens to him," Rose said to Ann, "I couldn't stand it." The family decided to tell Joe about the tragedy the next morning. In the meantime, they tried to maintain a facade of normalcy and to convince him that all of the television sets were broken so he would not hear the news reports.

Rose barely slept that night and looked tired and drawn as she left the house the next morning to attend a special mass that she had requested at St. Francis Xavier's. But Rose's fellow communicants remember Rose sitting up straight in the pew, her head held high. Teddy, Eunice, and Ann also were there but left at the end of the mass. Rose remained for a second mass.

Rose could not bear to tell Joe the horrible news, so Teddy disclosed the tragedy to his father after breakfast. Although the doctor told Rose that Joe was capable of making the trip to Washington, D.C., for his son's funeral, he stayed at home. An old friend, Father John Cavanaugh, stayed at the Kennedys' house and comforted Joe while the family went to the funeral.

When Rose arrived at the White House, her son-in-law, Sargent Shriver, greeted her and showed her up to the Lincoln bedroom, her favorite guest room. She then lost her composure for the first time, collapsing in Shriver's arms. She quickly straightened up, though, after her son-in-law remarked how well she had handled herself. "What do people expect you to do?" Rose said. "[Y]ou can't just weep in a corner."

Leaders from 92 countries—including French president Charles de Gaulle and Ethiopian emperor Haile Selassie—attended John Kennedy's funeral on November 25, 1963, and millions of people lined the route from the U.S. Capitol to St. Matthew's Cathedral. Rose was too weak and exhausted to walk in the somber procession, but at St. Matthew's she took a seat next to Jackie in the first pew. Rose noted in her memoirs that she did not receive Communion during the funeral mass because she had taken it at an earlier mass that morning.

At the grave site at Arlington National Cemetery in Virginia, Rose was praying so intently that when Bobby tried to hand her the torch to light the eternal flame by Jack's tombstone, Rose did not see him. Gail Cameron

The faces of the members of the Kennedy family are etched in grief as the honor guard lowers John Kennedy's flag-draped coffin into the ground. President Kennedy was interred at Arlington National Cemetery in Virginia, where an eternal flame marks his grave.

reports that "once only, Rose removed a handkerchief from her purse and quickly reached under her veil and wiped her eyes."

After a short reception at the White House, Rose flew back to Hyannis Port to be with Joe. According to Cameron, when Rose stepped down from the plane in Hyannis Port, "her face was deathly pale; her eyes were fixed on the ground; she clenched her hands tightly together in front of her—as if in constant prayer." The strain of the last four days clearly showed.

Thanksgiving was three days later. By Thursday, most of the family gathered in Hyannis Port at the Kennedys' house for their traditional Thanksgiving dinner. There was even a touch football game before the dinner—a traditional activity in the Kennedy family. Joe and Rose took their places at the huge dining-room table, and as Rose described in her memoirs, "We had the Thanksgiving celebration, with every one of us hiding the grief that gnawed at us and doing our best to make it a day of peace, optimism, and thanks for the blessings that were still left to us."

A few weeks later, Rose and Joe moved down to their Palm Beach home for the winter months. In January 1964, less than two months after Jack's death, Rose began attending memorials for her slain son throughout the country. The first major memorial was in Boston, where Cardinal Cushing offered a solemn high mass for John at Holy Cross Cathedral. The Boston Symphony Orchestra performed a concert during the mass, and 1,800 people filled the church where John had served as an altar boy. Rose was especially touched by the music the conductor, Erich Leinsdorf, chose—Mozart's Requiem in D Minor. Like John's unfulfilled mission in public life, Mozart's requiem was left unfinished because of the composer's death at the age of 35.

All over the world, streets, libraries, and other buildings were being dedicated to the memory of John Kennedy, including the Kennedy Center for the Performing Arts in Washington, D.C., the Avenue du President Kennedy in Paris, the John F. Kennedy Memorial Library at the Haile Selassie I University in Ethiopia, and the John F. Kennedy Memorial Library in Cambridge, Massachusetts.

In December 1964, Rose Kennedy joins West German dignitaries at the opening of the John F. Kennedy Memorial Exhibition in Bonn, West Germany. She joined the exhibition's three-week European tour, granting those who visited the exhibition the opportunity to see a member of the Kennedy family.

In June 1964, Rose went on a three-week European tour with the John F. Kennedy Memorial Library exhibit of her son's memorabilia. Rose admitted to reporters at Kennedy Airport in New York City that holding and being near John's personal articles would be difficult, but according to Cameron, Rose insisted on going. She explained, "Everyone likes to see a member of the family, and we are doing it because people have been so very generous in their tributes." The exhibit is now on permanent display at the Kennedy Memorial Library at Harvard University.

In the meantime, Bobby decided to run for the U.S. Senate in New York that fall, and Rose once again hit the campaign trail for one of her sons. She even spent her 50th wedding anniversary stumping for Bobby in Newburgh, New York.

Rose was particularly helpful in answering the charge that Bobby was a political "carpetbagger," an out-of-stater who had no business running for the Senate in New York. Bobby and Rose devised a way to handle the attacks. As Rose described in her memoirs, Bobby would bring up the issue in his speech and then turn to Rose and say, "'Tell them, Mother.' Which I would do, chapter and verse, about moving from Brookline to Riverdale and to Bronxville when Bobby was only 2 years old, and this was home to us for the next 14 years; and then even afterward we always had a residence in New York City." The strategy worked, and Bobby won the election by more than 700,000 votes. Rose proudly recalled in her memoirs that "when Congress reconvened that January of 1965 there were two Kennedy brothers present for roll call."

In 1968, Bobby enlisted Rose's help one more time. He had decided to seek the Democratic nomination for the presidency. At the age of 78, Rose again campaigned for the women's vote. She traveled to primaries in Indiana, Nebraska, Oregon, and California. In Indiana, Rose made her biggest political blunder during an interview with *Women's Wear Daily*. In response to a question about the

Rose Kennedy stumps for her son Robert in Utica, New York, during his 1964 senate campaign. She greeted more than 3,000 people in a receiving line after her speech.

Kennedy millions and the advantage it gave Bobby, Rose lost her patience. Instead of giving her usual response of "Please don't talk about money," Rose said, "It's our money and we're free to spend it any way we please. It's part of this campaign business. If you have money, you spend it to win. And the more you can afford, the more you'll spend." Rose shrewdly joked about her blunder later in Oregon, though, by saying, "I don't talk about high finances anymore—if I did, they'd send me home tonight."

After winning the California primary on June 4, 1968, an elated but physically exhausted Bobby raised his hand to the ecstatic supporters who had squeezed into the Embassy Ballroom of the Ambassador Hotel in Los Angeles. He thanked his supporters and exhorted, "So on to Chicago, and let's win there." As he headed out of the crowded room through the hotel's kitchen, a young man leaned over the senator's aides and from a distance of only a few feet fired a revolver at Kennedy's head. Aides grabbed the gunman, Sirhan Sirhan, who continued to fire wildly. Four more people were wounded. Reports of the shooting spread back to the ballroom, where the horrified crowd learned that their candidate had been shot.

Rose had just flown back to Hyannis Port from California earlier that day to watch the election results on TV with Joe. They learned of the assassination attempt the next morning when she woke up to go to church. Ann received a call about the shooting in the middle of the night but had decided not to wake either Rose or Joe with the grave news.

Rose learned from television reports that Bobby was still alive. He had been shot three times. Bullets were embedded in his neck and midbrain; a third had grazed his forehead. Teddy, who was in San Francisco, flew to Los Angeles and rushed to the Hospital of the Good Samaritan. He called his mother to tell her that there seemed to be very little hope. Bobby, having fallen into a coma after brain surgery, was barely clinging to life. Rose insisted on attending mass at St. Francis Xavier that morning even

Rose Kennedy joins Robert in Omaha, Nebraska, to campaign for votes in the 1968 Nebraska presidential primary. She also traveled to Indiana, Oregon, and California on behalf of her son.

On June 6, 1968, Robert Kennedy, Jr., escorts his grandmother into St. Patrick's Cathedral to attend the funeral service for Robert Kennedy, who had been slain by an assassin, Sirhan Sirhan, in Los Angeles.

though she knew she would have to face reporters and photographers. At the church she scolded cameramen for making too much noise and ordered them out of the church.

Rose wrote in her memoirs that later, back at the house, she "kept busy in my room, sorting, rearranging, doing anything to keep busy, because I had to keep moving." The news from Teddy in Los Angeles grew progressively worse. The next morning, on Thursday, June 6, 1968, Bobby passed away at the age of 42. He left 10 children, and his wife, Ethel, was pregnant with their 11th child. Again, Rose went to mass.

Later that day, Rose flew to New York City, where Bobby's funeral would be held. After stopping at Bergdorf-Goodman to purchase some mourning clothes, she joined other relatives at St. Patrick's Cathedral to wait for Bobby's coffin to arrive from California. That night, more than 100,000 people came to St. Patrick's to pay their respects to her son.

The next day at the funeral, Teddy delivered a moving eulogy and did so, as Rose wrote in her memoirs, "with dignity, simplicity, eloquence, and grace. His three brothers were gone. His father would go soon, as he knew. And he was a credit to all of them." Describing Rose's appearance at the funeral, Cameron writes, "As she looked out at her youngest child and sole surviving son, she appeared to be holding back tears. Her face wore a half-smile of resignation. But she did not cry."

In the months following Bobby's death, Rose traveled to Europe once and assisted Teddy in raising money to cover Bobby's campaign debt of more than $3 million. Teddy organized the dinners—usually $500 to $1,000 a plate—and Rose appeared at some of the affairs to give her own reflections on Bobby. "When I think of him," Rose told a group of Democratic leaders at the Sheraton Plaza in Washington, D.C., "I think of children. His personal life was filled with children. How sad we are, that we shall never see Bobby again. What joy he brought us. What an aching void he has left in our hearts."

Despite her personal grief, Rose continued to keep up with her many charities and social obligations. Throughout the 1970s, she often appeared on the society pages of local newspapers for such events as dedicating a new school for the mentally retarded, promoting her line of Flame of Hope perfumes (also to benefit the mentally retarded), or attending a major art gallery opening.

The publicity that the Kennedys have received through the years, though, has not always been flattering. Just over a year after Bobby died, another tragedy struck the Kennedy family. On July 18, 1969, Teddy was involved in a puzzling car accident, and a young woman who was riding with him was killed.

Unaware of the incident, Rose was going ahead with her plans to attend a book bazaar at St. Francis Xavier the afternoon of July 19 to autograph books about her sons. Teddy called Rose just before she left, to ask her not to go because reporters would deluge her with questions. Rose stayed home, learning the details of the accident that almost ended Teddy's political career.

Teddy was driving Mary Jo Kopechne, a campaign worker, home from a party on Chappaquiddick Island on

Attired in a white fur hat and a lavender knitted dress, Rose Kennedy passes out autographed cards to purchasers of candles from the Flame of Hope Foundation, one of her many charities.

the night of July 18, when his car ran off Dyke Bridge and plunged into the water upside down. Teddy managed to escape but waited a full eight hours before reporting the accident to the police. Mary Jo had drowned. As Gail Cameron has noted, the "whole event reeked of duplicity and fraud—and from a Kennedy, the family in which a nation had once invested its dreams and hopes, the event was even more shocking."

The newspapers were relentless in their pursuit of the truth surrounding Teddy's relationship with Mary Jo and how the Kennedy family was reacting to the tragedy. Rose's last surviving son appeared to have ruined the family's legacy. Political advisers sought for ways to quell the bad publicity. Teddy gave a television address in which he asked for the advice of his constituents, the people of Massachusetts. But the speech came off as a feeble ploy to save Teddy's political career.

Rose had hoped that Teddy would run for president in 1972. He was considered a strong candidate in 1968 after his brother Bobby's death. But that would have to wait. After losing Joe, Jr., Kick, Jack, and Bobby, and the long illness of her husband, Joe, Rose had to bear the weight of an incident that jeopardized Teddy's political future. From all accounts, Rose did not display any heartbreak or depression after the Chappaquiddick episode. She maintained her stoicism in the face of the public scrutiny. Cameron noted that Rose still spoke with authority, claiming, "I'm sure Ted can rise above all this," and she even kept her sense of humor when she disputed reports that she was 80 years old. The now-79-year-old Rose found such inaccuracy "very unfair."

Rose wrote to Mary Jo's parents expressing her sympathy and telling them that she understood—after losing her own daughter, Kathleen, at the age of 28—how much they were suffering. Later that year, when Rose was in New York City, she learned that the Kopechnes were also in the city, and she invited them to the Kennedys' apartment. As Rose described in her memoirs, "[W]e talked about the joys and sorrows that life brings all of us."

Teddy was reelected to the Senate in 1970, but the questions surrounding the Chappaquiddick incident will always haunt him and hinder any attempts he may make at seeking higher office.

Joe Kennedy's health had progressively declined. By autumn of 1969, he was nearly helpless, unable even to feed himself most of the time. On November 18, 1969, surrounded by his surviving children and his beloved wife, Joe died. Rose was kneeling by his bedside, holding his hand. In her memoirs, she lovingly wrote, "Next to Almighty God, I had loved him—do love him—with all my heart, all my soul, all my mind."

Rose requested a special funeral mass, at which the priests wore white—to signify joy—instead of the traditional purple or black vestments of mourning. At the funeral, Teddy offered deep thanks to his cousin Ann for her loyalty to Joe and read a prayer written by Rose: "I thank thee, O my God, with all my heart for all thou has done for me. I thank thee, especially, for my husband who with your help has made possible so many joys and such great happiness in my life." Joe was buried in the family plot at Holyhood Cemetery, not far from the Beals Street house in Brookline where he and Rose had started their family 55 years earlier.

On January 5, 1970, Senator Edward Kennedy faces a throng of reporters as he enters the Dukes County Court House for an inquest into the death of Mary Jo Kopechne, who had died when the senator's car plunged off a bridge into the water off Chappaquiddick Island, Massachusetts.

From the veranda of her house, Rose Kennedy waves to a crowd that had gathered outside the Kennedy compound in Hyannis Port, Massachusetts. Rose celebrated her 92nd birthday eight days after this photograph was taken in 1982.

8

The Kennedy Legacy

"IT'S A GOOD LIFE," Rose has said. "God does not send us a cross any heavier than we can bear." She expressed this sentiment after the Chappaquiddick incident, one of the several tragedies to strike the Kennedys during the 1960s—a decade that began with so much promise when her son John won the presidency. Rose's fortitude in the face of so much disappointment and sorrow has today won her the admiration of many.

Rose has been out of the public eye since the mid-1970s because her physical condition has progressively deteriorated. Since 1985, she has remained in Hyannis Port, where she is cared for by nurses around the clock. Weighing less than 100 pounds and with failing eyesight, the Kennedy matriarch requires full-time nursing. Confined to a wheelchair after several strokes, Rose still follows a regular schedule. She says the rosary every day, and on Sunday mornings a priest says Mass in her living room. She listens to the news, has her hair done each week, and loves to hear stories about her children and grandchildren. But

In August 1981, Rose Kennedy joins her family during a clambake at the Kennedy compound in Hyannis Port. The family held the event to raise campaign funds for Senator Edward Kennedy.

Rose's image will always be that of a woman of intelligence, stamina, and vitality. And she remains the matriarch of a family whose accomplishments are nothing less than extraordinary to this day.

In 1990, Rose turned 100 years old. The family planned a special party to celebrate her centennial. The party was held a week earlier than her July 22 birthday so that it would coincide with the presentation of awards by the Joseph P. Kennedy, Jr., Foundation to those performing exemplary work in fighting mental retardation. Her children—Eunice, Patricia, Jean, and Teddy—and most of her 28 grandchildren and 22 great-grandchildren attended the celebration. Her daughter Rosemary, who remained in the care of the convent in Wisconsin, was unable to make the trip to the party. The guests gathered under a large tent to watch a film of Rose's life, which Teddy narrated. Singer Maureen McGovern performed some of Rose's favorite songs and led the gathering in singing "Happy Birthday."

The torch of the Kennedy legacy has now passed to Rose's grandchildren, who have begun to forge notable public and private lives. Joe Kennedy III, Bobby's oldest son, has won the congressional seat once occupied by his uncle John and his great-grandfather Johnny Fitzgerald. Patrick Kennedy, Teddy's youngest son, serves as a representative in the Rhode Island State House. Robert Kennedy, Jr., is a staff attorney for the Natural Resources Defense Council. Maria Shriver is a noted television journalist. John Kennedy, Jr., is an assistant district attorney in New York City. His older sister, Caroline Kennedy Schlossberg, cowrote *In Our Defense* (1991), a book about the Bill of Rights. And Teddy Kennedy, Jr., who overcame the loss of one leg to bone cancer in his youth, is studying environmental science at Yale University.

In her memoirs, Rose provided the following advice to her grandchildren:

> I hope they will realize where they came from and how they happen to be where they are. They came—on the Kennedy-Fitzgerald side—from ancestors who were quite poor and disadvantaged through no fault of their own but who had the imagination, the resolve, the intelligence, and the energy to seek a new, better world for themselves and their families. And had the willingness to work as hard as they had to, and suffer whatever had to be suffered, and to look to the future and plan for whatever could be planned, and to seize gratefully on any piece of good luck that came their way. If none came, to look for it, look for opportunity.

The story of the Kennedy family is certainly one of opportunities seized, risks taken, and challenges overcome. The price this family paid for such accomplishment

Rose Kennedy rides in a Parade held in Hyannis, Massachusetts, to honor her 90th birthday in 1980. Her indomitable spirit has helped her family overcome their misfortunes and has ensured that the Kennedy legacy will be passed down to the next generation.

and stature has been a great one, but not one lost upon the new generation of Kennedys. Chris Lawford, Patricia Kennedy Lawford's son, put it simply when writing about his grandmother Rose: "There's no baloney with Grandma. She often reminds me that life is not a bowl of cherries, and that you have to do a lot of things you don't really want to do. And that often you don't get to do what you want when you want. And there are plenty of times when you're going to have to put your head down and just get through it. And she's right."

Further Reading

Cameron, Gail. *Rose: A Biography of Rose Kennedy.* New York: Putnam, 1971.

Cutler, John Henry. *"Honey Fitz": Three Steps to the White House.* Indianapolis: Bobbs-Merrill, 1962.

Gibson, Barbara. *Life with Rose Kennedy.* New York: Warner Books, 1986.

Goodwin, Doris Kearns. *The Fitzgeralds and the Kennedys.* New York: St. Martin's Press, 1987.

Kennedy, Rose Fitzgerald. *Times to Remember.* Garden City, NY: Doubleday, 1974.

Koskoff, David E. *Joseph P. Kennedy: A Life and Times.* Englewood Cliffs, NJ: Prentice-Hall, 1974.

Krock, Arthur. *Memoirs: Sixty Years on the Firing Line.* New York: Funk & Wagnalls, 1968.

Martin, Ralph G. *A Hero for Our Time.* New York: Macmillan, 1983.

Parmet, Herbert S. *Jack: The Struggles of John F. Kennedy.* New York: Dial Press, 1980.

Whalen, Richard J. *The Founding Father: The Story of Joseph P. Kennedy.* New York: New American Library, 1964.

Rose Kennedy's Family Tree

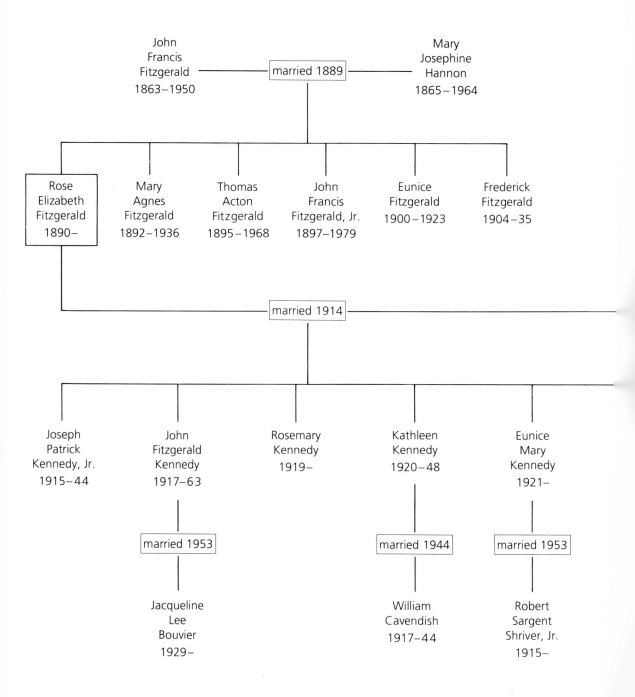

John Francis Fitzgerald 1863–1950 — married 1889 — Mary Josephine Hannon 1865–1964

- Rose Elizabeth Fitzgerald 1890–
- Mary Agnes Fitzgerald 1892–1936
- Thomas Acton Fitzgerald 1895–1968
- John Francis Fitzgerald, Jr. 1897–1979
- Eunice Fitzgerald 1900–1923
- Frederick Fitzgerald 1904–35

married 1914

- Joseph Patrick Kennedy, Jr. 1915–44
- John Fitzgerald Kennedy 1917–63
- Rosemary Kennedy 1919–
- Kathleen Kennedy 1920–48
- Eunice Mary Kennedy 1921–

married 1953 — Jacqueline Lee Bouvier 1929–

married 1944 — William Cavendish 1917–44

married 1953 — Robert Sargent Shriver, Jr. 1915–

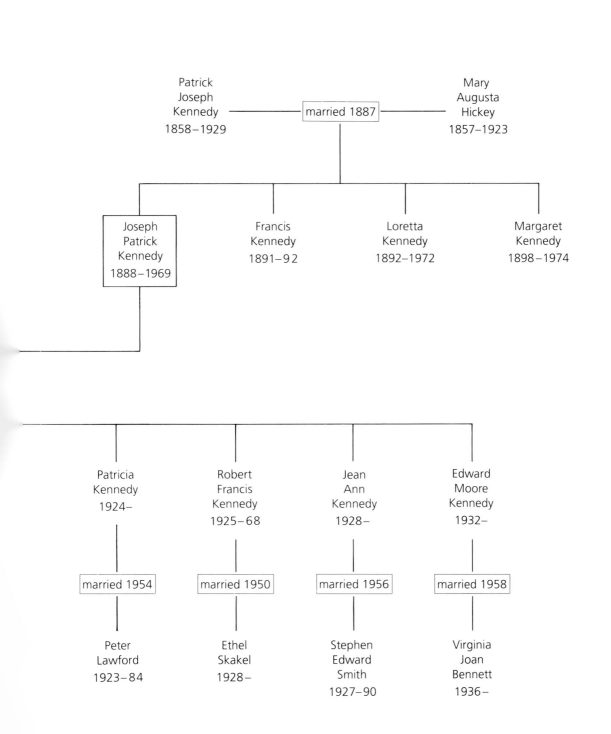

Patrick Joseph Kennedy 1858–1929 — married 1887 — Mary Augusta Hickey 1857–1923

Joseph Patrick Kennedy 1888–1969

Francis Kennedy 1891–92

Loretta Kennedy 1892–1972

Margaret Kennedy 1898–1974

Patricia Kennedy 1924– — married 1954 — Peter Lawford 1923–84

Robert Francis Kennedy 1925–68 — married 1950 — Ethel Skakel 1928–

Jean Ann Kennedy 1928– — married 1956 — Stephen Edward Smith 1927–90

Edward Moore Kennedy 1932– — married 1958 — Virginia Joan Bennett 1936–

Chronology

1890	Born Rose Elizabeth Fitzgerald in Boston, Massachusetts, on July 22
1897	Moves with family to West Concord, Massachusetts
1906	John Fitzgerald begins first term as mayor of Boston; Rose graduates from Dorchester High School
1908–9	Attends Sacred Heart Convent in Blumenthal, Holland
1911	Celebrates formal debut on January 2
1914	Marries Joseph Patrick Kennedy on October 7
1915	Gives birth to son Joseph Patrick, Jr.
1917	Gives birth to son John Fitzgerald
1919	Gives birth to daughter Rosemary
1920	Gives birth to daughter Kathleen
1921	Gives birth to daughter Eunice Mary
1924	Gives birth to daughter Patricia
1925	Gives birth to son Robert Francis
1926	Moves with family from Brookline, Massachusetts, to Riverdale, New York
1928	Gives birth to daughter Jean Ann; moves with family to Bronxville, New York
1932	Gives birth to son Edward Moore
1938	Sails to London to join her husband, who is serving as U.S. ambassador to the United Kingdom
1939	Attends coronation of Pope Pius XII; returns to the United States after the United Kingdom declares war on Germany
1944	Joseph P. Kennedy, Jr., killed in action; the Kennedy family establishes the Joseph P. Kennedy, Jr., Foundation
1946	Campaigns for son John Kennedy in his successful campaign for U.S. Congress

1948	Kathleen Kennedy dies in airplane crash in France
1950	John Fitzgerald dies in Boston
1952	Campaigns for son John in his successful campaign for U.S. Senate
1960	Travels to Democratic National Convention in Los Angeles, California, to watch son John nominated as that party's presidential candidate
1961	Attends presidential inauguration of John F. Kennedy on January 20
1962	Campaigns for son Edward in his successful campaign for U.S. Senate
1963	John F. Kennedy assassinated on November 22
1964	Rose Kennedy accompanies European tour of John F. Kennedy Library exhibit; campaigns for son Robert in his successful campaign for U.S. Senate
1968	Robert F. Kennedy dies on June 6 from gunshot wounds inflicted by an assassin
1969	Edward Kennedy's political career jeopardized because of Chappaquiddick incident; Joseph P. Kennedy, Sr., dies
1970s	Rose Kennedy makes appearances for various charities, such as the Flame of Hope
1980s	Withdraws from the public eye
1990	Celebrates her 100th birthday at Hyannis Port, Massachusetts

Index

Susan Beale Simonelli, a freelance writer, was born and raised in Birmingham, Michigan. She and her husband, Tony, reside in Princeton, New Jersey, with their son, Mario. Ms. Simonelli attended the University of Michigan and is currently completing a master's degree in public policy and administration at Columbia University. She has worked as an international trade analyst for a law firm in Washington, D.C., and as a consultant to the World Bank on projects involving agricultural development policy in Algeria and Tunisia. Most recently, Ms. Simonelli served as a research analyst for the New York City Charter Revision Commission.

Vito Perrone is Director of Teacher Education and Chair of Teaching, Curriculum, and Learning Environments at Harvard University. He has previous experience as a public school teacher, a university professor of history, education, and peace studies (University of North Dakota), and as dean of the New School and the Center for Teaching and Learning (both at the University of North Dakota). Dr. Perrone has written extensively about such issues as educational equity, humanities curriculum, progressive education, and evaluation. His most recent books are: *A Letter to Teachers: Reflections on Schooling and the Art of Teaching*; *Enlarging Student Assessment in Schools*; *Working Papers: Reflections on Teachers, Schools, and Communities*; *Visions of Peace*; and *Johanna Knudsen Miller: A Pioneer Teacher*.